U2

Past, Present, Future

BonoAdamLarryTheEdgeBonoAdamLarryTheEdge
AdamLarryTheEdgeBonoAdamLarryTheEdgeBono
LarryTheEdgeBonoAdamLarryTheEdgeBonoAdam
TheEdgeBonoAdamLarryTheEdgeBonoAdamLarry
BonoAdamLarryTheEdgeBonoAdamLarryTheEdge
AdamLarryTheEdgeBonoAdamLarryTheEdgeBono
LarryTheEdgeBonoAdamLarryTheEdgeBonoAdam
TheEdgeBonoAdamLarryTheEdgeBonoAdamLarry
BonoAdamLarryTheEdgeBonoAdamLarryTheEdge
AdamLarryTheEdgeBonoAdamLarryTheEdgeBono
LarryTheEdgeBonoAdamLarryTheEdgeBonoAdam
TheEdgeBonoAdamLarryTheEdgeBonoAdamLarry
BonoAdamLarryTheEdgeBonoAdamLarryTheEdge
AdamLarryTheEdgeBonoAdamLarryTheEdgeBono
LarryTheEdgeBonoAdamLarryTheEdgeBonoAdam
TheEdgeBonoAdamLarryTheEdgeBonoAdamLarry
BonoAdamLarryTheEdgeBonoAdamLarryTheEdge
AdamLarryTheEdgeBonoAdamLarryTheEdgeBono
LarryTheEdgeBonoAdamLarryTheEdgeBonoAdam
TheEdgeBonoAdamLarryTheEdgeBonoAdamLarry
BonoAdamLarryTheEdgeBonoAdamLarryTheEdge
AdamLarryTheEdgeBonoAdamLarryTheEdgeBono
LarryTheEdgeBonoAdamLarryTheEdgeBonoAdam
TheEdgeBonoAdamLarryTheEdgeBonoAdamLarry
BonoAdamLarryTheEdgeBonoAdamLarryTheEdge
AdamLarryTheEdgeBonoAdamLarryTheEdgeBono
LarryTheEdgeBonoAdamLarryTheEdgeBonoAdam
TheEdgeBonoAdamLarryTheEdgeBonoAdamLarry

U2 OCTOBER
U2 OCTOBER
1764103
1761670
U2•BOY
262
BF

EARTH
SUCKS
U2
WAR
U2 WAR
www.u2.com
UNION SQUARE
CENTER
AT ORANGE
MILLS
ORLANDO
WORLD® RESORT
INTERSCOPE RECORDS
ISLAND
UMe
UNIVERSAL
A UNIVERSAL MUSIC COMPANY
© 2008 Universal-Island Records Limited

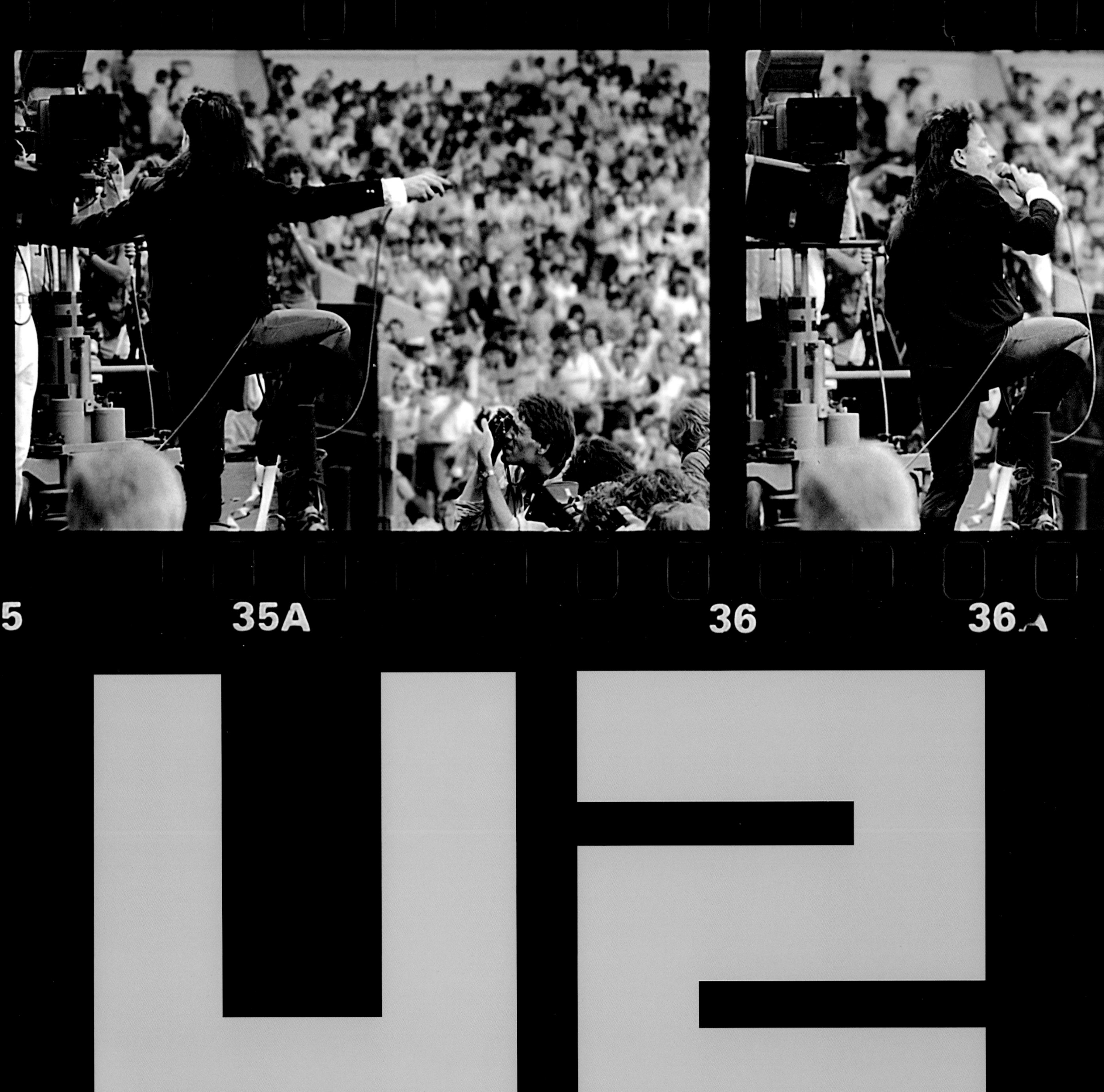
35A
36
U2

Contents

TEXT BY
ERNESTO ASSANTE

EDITED BY
VALERIA MANFERTO DE FABIANIS

EDITORIAL COORDINATION
LAURA ACCOMAZZO

GRAPHIC DESIGN
PAOLA PIACCO

INTRODUCTION

SEPTEMBER 25, 1976...

The date was September 25, 1976. That was the day Larry Mullen Jr. met up with the people who had responded to a note he had posted on the bulletin bord at Mount Temple Comprehensive School, about creating a band. His father, Larry Mullen Sr., had suggested he look for people who might share his passion, by posting a note. Six people responded, ready to play in the young drummer's kitchen. Brothers David and Dick Evans and their friend Adam Clayton. Ivan McCormick and Peter Martin, two other friends of Larry's, also showed up. Then there was Paul Hewson. They all attended Mount Temple and, for one reason or another, none of them had a great future at the school, and a few of them had gone through huge family tragedies. Larry and Paul had both lost their mothers and the others simply couldn't find their place in the world. For all of them, music was a way out, a window to the world. It was life. No one really knew how to play an instrument but they had a punk rock soul, which was ignited in those weeks, pushing them to pick one up and get on stage, in spite of their lack of skill. Their desire to play was strong and so was their energy. "I never thought we were doing anything important, to tell you the truth," remembers Larry, "I liked the idea of making some noise with the others. I didn't have any particular expectations; we wanted to have fun. But it only took a few practices for everyone to get that what we were doing was different. We weren't simply doing something in our free time after school." Larry was the first to arrive. "I had an electric base, a great reason to be a part of it." Then David and Dick Evans arrived "with our yellow guitar, like a Flying V, that Dick built himself," recalls David. Then Paul arrived, who said, "I didn't even bring a guitar. Reggie Manuel convinced me to go and took me on his scooter. I was sitting behind him, I couldn't bring one." Then Ivan McCormick and Peter Martin arrived. They didn't play much, it was more like an afternoon chatting and getting to know each other, to see if they could be part of the same dream. But they all liked each other; they strummed their guitars, admired Larry's drums in the corner of the kitchen, the songs mentioned by David, Paul's roughneck look and they scheduled the next practice. And they did it again and again. They asked their teachers at Mount Temple for a place to practice on Wednesday afternoons, the only day of the week they got out early, so that they could rehearse at school. And they continued month after month – mangled songs, take after take, playing basic instruments. But their fame grew. At school, they became "the ones in the band". They chose the name "Feedback" and they debuted in the school gym with a playlist of only two songs, Peter Framption's "Show me the Way" and The Bay City Rollers' "Bye Bye Baby". But it went well and after that first show, they knew they didn't want to do anything else. However, to get better, they

4-5 *October*, *War* and *Boy* were the band's debut albums that earned them recognition outside their country.

would need to be more committed, so they doubled their rehearsal time. They didn't just practice for an hour on Wednesdays, but also on Saturdays. Peter Martin left the project immediately and Ivan McCormick continued for a few weeks but then he, too, left the band (a mistake he regretted for many years, until he finally wrote the book, *Killing Bono,* which was later made into a film). Other concerts at other schools allowed them to refine their style and build up their playlist, which was still all covers but more in line with the era's punk rock flavor. However, more importantly, it allowed them to become Feedback, the band. Perhaps the music wasn't yet all that great, but the band had good stage presence, great energy, and a strong image. "Yes, our look wasn't bad. Adam was cool, even though he didn't really know how to play bass; Larry was good-looking and blond behind the drum set and I did the best I could; Bono was crazy on stage. Basically, we were pretty bad; we didn't know how to close songs, Bono would forget the words, and Adam was not in time; I improvised, trying to keep up with Larry's timing," remembers The Edge. Yet, slowly but surely, things got better. Actually, Bono wrote his first song and the band began to follow him; their repertoire changed and they became more confident, their sets had more new, original pieces and fewer covers. And each band member found his place, sound, and identity. David Evans became "The Edge" and Paul Hewson became "Bono Vox". They changed the name of the band too, calling it The Hype and they continued to practice, play and gain experience. In March 1978, they got their first big break. On St. Patrick's Day, the band, now called U2 (a name chosen from a list of six suggestions by Steve Averill, a member of punk rock band The Radiators, and a friend of Clayton's), entered a competition in Limerick. They chose U2 because it was ambiguous, open to many interpretations and, as The Edge said, "In the end, it was the name we disliked the least." Dick Evans was the last to leave the band, but he didn't leave rock; he found music that was more to his taste with the Virgin Prunes and U2 became a four-piece ensemble that very day. They won the competition, a five hundred pound prize, and some studio time, enough to record their first demo for CBS in Ireland. Adam Clayton had been acting as manager until that time, booking concerts in schools and small clubs. But things changed when Paul McGuinness entered the picture – he had been introduced to the band by journalist Bill Graham. After the competition in Limerick, he took over and pushed the band toward releasing its first album, simply entitled *Three*, which came out in September 1979 and put the band on the Irish charts for the first time. In December, the band performed in London for the first time, without much success. Two months later, they released their second single, "Another Day," and that set everything in motion.

6-7 A series of shots showing Bono on the Live Aid stage at London's Wembley Stadium in 1985. That performance opened the road to worldwide fame for the band.

10-11 Adam Clayton, Larry Mullen, Bono and The Edge in a 2015 photo. The Irish band had entered its fourth decade, with a career full of success.

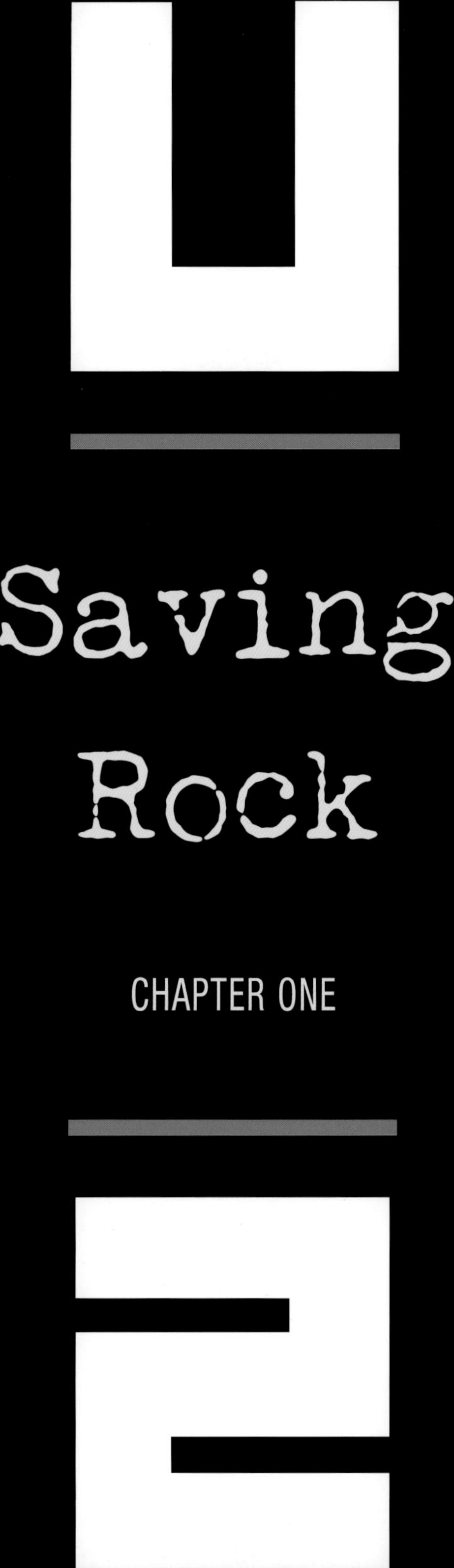

Saving Rock

CHAPTER ONE

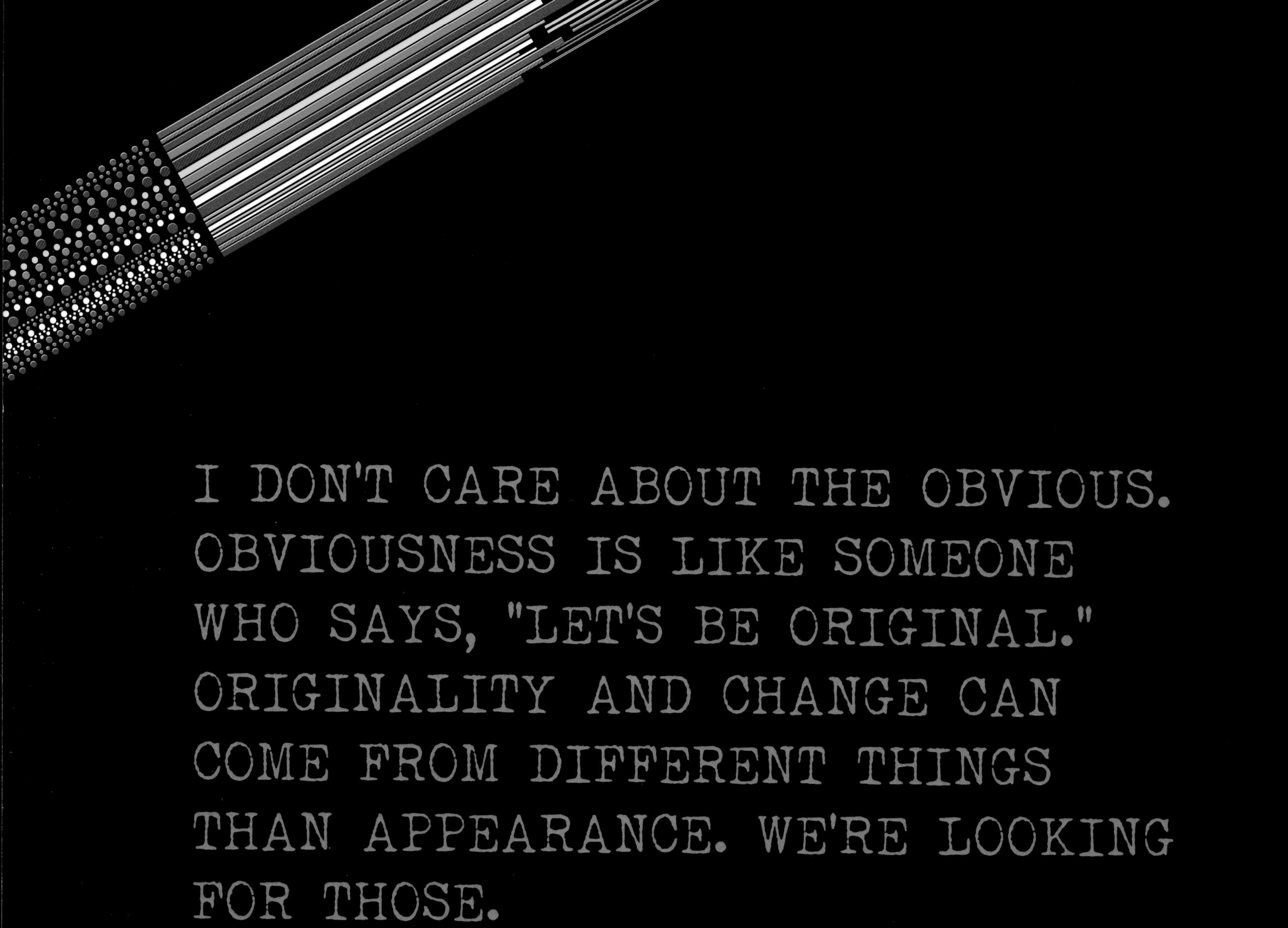

I DON'T CARE ABOUT THE OBVIOUS. OBVIOUSNESS IS LIKE SOMEONE WHO SAYS, "LET'S BE ORIGINAL." ORIGINALITY AND CHANGE CAN COME FROM DIFFERENT THINGS THAN APPEARANCE. WE'RE LOOKING FOR THOSE.

In the beginning, it seemed like any standard rock fairy tale: a note is placed on a school bulletin board, the kids meet up, play their first songs and do their first concerts. But there is something different about the tale when U2 tells it. That is because U2 was not in search of just success, fame or fans. The band had a bigger, richer and more complex aim – and that was to save rock.

They wanted to save rock from death – death by asphyxiation, irrelevance, corruption and abandonment. When the 1980s arrived, after the hard-hitting punk period, it seemed all was lost. Electronic keyboards took the place of electric guitars, drums were replaced by drum machines and the meaning of rock seemed to have been lost, with the public splintering into thousands of different tribes. It wasn't just the old clash between mods and rockers; the diaspora was all-encompassing and unstoppable. The public was divided by genre, sub-genre, clothing, make-up, and shoes and each one corresponded to a sound and a style. Rock, the extraordinary "way of doing things" that combined freedom, creativity and desire was reduced to a simulacrum of itself with its heavy metal hairdos. Then the new wave era was born, and U2 represented a traditionalist branch of it that didn't experiment with futuristic elements, like Talking Heads did or The Clash tried to do, for example. It seemed that U2 wanted nothing more than to pick up where it had left off, take the spirit of punk and immerse it in the visionary rock of the 1970s, outlawing electronic keyboards and precision drummers, bringing electricity back to guitars. They didn't want digital coldness; they were looking for heart and soul, emotion and feeling.

This is what the music of their early years was all about. "We weren't just looking for success. To be clear, we wanted to be successful, we wanted people to listen to us and we wanted our records to make the charts, but it wasn't our main goal. What we were working on, what grew with us, was the relationship with the public and the relationship they had with our music. We promised a lot. We promised honesty, rebellion, strength, movement and we weren't afraid of the expectations of the fans. If they wanted the world, we were ready to give it to them," said Bono. In speaking to us, Bono remembered his early days, when in his opinion, everything revolved around one spark, "Yes, a spark. We knew we had something to say, even in the beginning, when none of us was even remotely good enough to imagine a future in music. Yet we had that spark and we knew it. We saw it when we played live. There was no chance of us being as good as other bands, the others were technically better and more prepared, but we had an effect on the audience that the others, even with their technical abilities, could not achieve. We were insecure, but we relied on that insecurity and knew our weaknesses and worked around them; we always tried to be different from the others and find the best in ourselves," he recalled.

1976-1983

But who were these four guys who released three consecutive albums – *Boy*, *October* and *War* – that carried them to the top of the all-time greatest of rock 'n' roll? Even today, those records are part of the backbone of their concerts. And indeed, the songs are still on the lips of millions of fans all over the world. They were words and sounds that, for forty years, have represented the way U2 has shown the kids of the future a way to work out and solve problems they face in their early twenties. Times change, but the struggle to get through adolescence and take on the world never changes. And there is nothing better than rock as a key tool to take on this challenge. So, reviving rock meant transforming it once again into a vehicle for understanding and facing the times. It was far from the self-reference machine of the progressive rock of the 1970s or a machine that turned the nihilistic and destructive fury of punk rock into something positive. It was a machine that found energy to go forward by returning to its origins, to the virtual launch pad, to Bob Dylan, the Beatles and The Who. It was meant to give rock back its salvific function, if salvation meant getting away from your average, mediocre or gray life. So who were these four guys who were ready to take on that responsibility?

12 A portrait of the group taken on the roof of the Cork Country Club Hotel in Cork, Ireland. In March 1980, the band had just been signed by Island Records and had begun working on their first album.

16-17 The very young band members pose for a picture at the Strand on the Green in London. In December 1979, they played in London's clubs, taking their music outside Ireland for the first time.

1976-1983

18-19 The band pose along the river bank in the Ringsend neighborhood of Dublin. In September 1979, the EP *Three*, released only in Ireland, made the charts.

19 December 14, 1979. The band played Dingwalls in London during a tour promoting the EP *Three*, in the U.K. and Ireland.

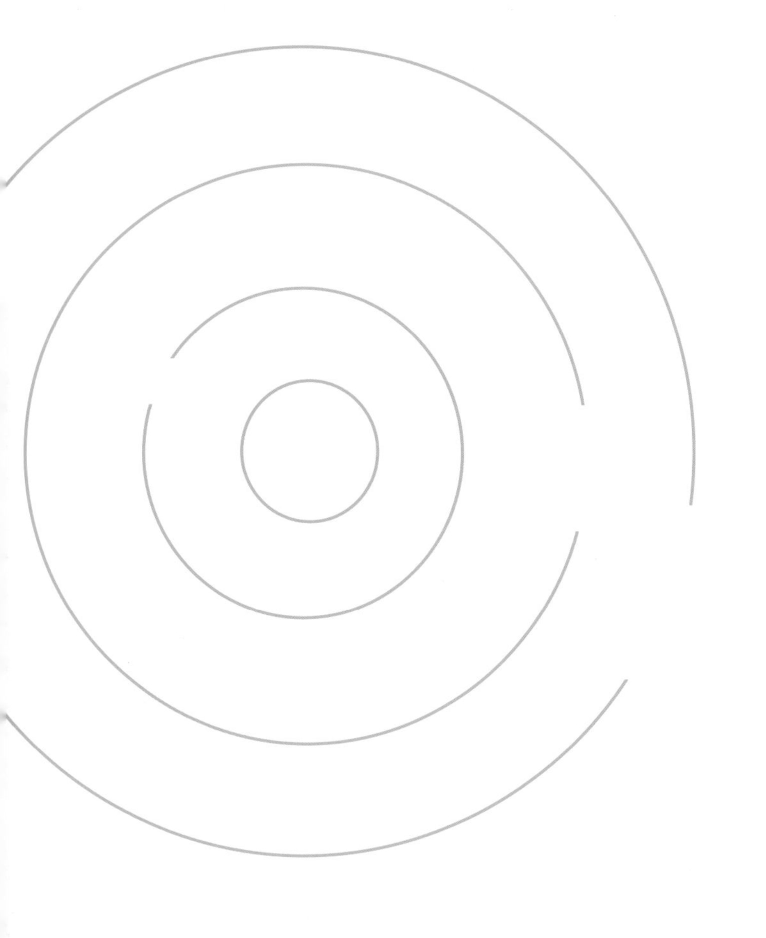

20-21 and 23 In October 1980, the band went on tour to promote *Boy*. The dates in Holland and Belgium were the first shows the band played on the European mainland.

> Bono

> Adam

> Larry

> The Edge

> Bono

Bono's real name is Paul David Hewson. He was born May 10, 1960, and he is the second son of Bob Hewson, a Catholic postal worker, and Iris Hewson, the daughter of Irish Protestants. When they married in August 1950, their differing religions created a bit of a problem, which was resolved with an agreement. On Sundays, Paul and his brother Norman went to Protestant church with their mother while their father went to Catholic mass. Paul's childhood was not easy. He was headstrong and rebellious; he always butted heads with his father, who was strict and inflexible. Every morning, his primary goal was to engage the entire world in battle. As an adolescent, he was kicked out of St. Patrick's Cathedral Choir School for throwing dog feces at his Spanish teacher. "I didn't have a good opinion of her and I suspect the feeling was mutual," he remembered. Perhaps you could say he was a "rambunctious kid". But in spite of his bad habits, young Paul did not hide his true ambitions of becoming an artist or at least putting his creativity to good use. At 12 years old, a passion for chess emerged and he studied strategies for the game, in books. Then, he decided to become a painter. He'd skip school to go to exhibitions at the Municipal Gallery of Modern Art in Dublin. And obviously, there was music. When Paul's grandmother died, Paul begged his parents to keep her piano. But the family sold it.

Paul's world was turned upside down in 1974. The night after his grandparents' wedding anniversary, his grandfather went to bed, had a heart attack and died. During the funeral, Paul's mother collapsed. She had had a brain hemorrhage. She was kept alive artificially for four days. But nothing could be done. Paul had a textbook reaction with a range of emotions: rage, aggression, insomnia, periods of amnesia, and suicidal thoughts. His only comfort was music. His brother, eight years his senior, played the guitar and introduced him to the Beatles, The Who and Jimi Hendrix. He taught Paul a few chords, especially those of songs by the Fab Four.

And just like that, he began a new life, with a new name, Bono Vox, a nickname given to him by Gavin Friday, his friend and shortly thereafter, a rock musician too, with the Virgin Prunes. And with the love of his life. In 1975, he started dating Alison Stewart, whom he later married, and one year later, he responded to Larry Mullen's note.

24 Bono in a portrait from October 1980. The nickname "Bono Vox" was given to him by his friend Fionan Martin Hanvey, known as Gavin Friday, of the Virgin Prunes.

25 Bono listened to the Beatles, the Clash and the Ramones in his youth.

HOLLYWOOD
SOUND HIRE
021 745 2194
HOLLYWOOD
SOUND HIRE

Adam Clayton was born May 13, 1960 in Chinnor, England to Brian and Jo Clayton. His father, an airline pilot, took the family to live first in Kenya and then, when Adam was five years old, to Ireland. There, Adam's parents met Dave's parents. The pair met, and played together occasionally, but they didn't become real friends until they responded to Larry's note.

His passion for music began in his teens, when he began to listen first to classical music and then to rock at St. Columba College, where he met John Leslie, who had a guitar and pushed him to buy a used one for five pounds. He decided to put a band together with John so he changed to the electric bass, which his parents bought him. Transferring from St. Columba, who expelled him for poor grades, to Mount Temple, changed his life forever.

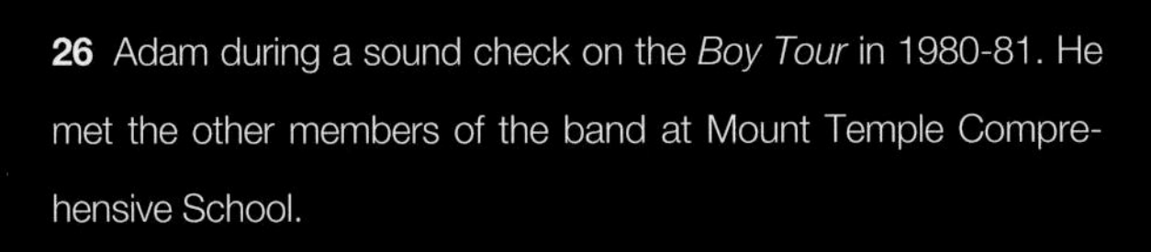

26 Adam during a sound check on the *Boy Tour* in 1980-81. He met the other members of the band at Mount Temple Comprehensive School.

> Larry

Larry, Lawrence Joseph Mullen, is slightly younger than Bono. He was born October 31, 1961. His father, Larry Sr., was a civil servant and his mother, Maureen, was a housewife. His childhood and teen years were not easy. His younger sister, Mary, died when he was only nine years old. And his mother was killed in a car accident in 1978. "These two events really scarred me and, in some way, pushed me towards the band," said Mullen. During high school, he was a sociable and fun guy; he was a fan of Elvis and loved rock 'n' roll. In high school, he met, and later married, Ann Acheson and they are still married. His musical journey began at eight years old when his family pushed him to take piano lessons. But his older sister, Cecilia, helped him find his niche when she gave him his first drum kit. Larry tried to take drum lessons, but they didn't last because he wasn't interested in playing in an 'orchestra' like the Post Office Workers Union Band or the Artane Boys Band, with whom he made his "debut". He loved rock, wanted a band, and because of this, he posted an announcement on the wall of Mount Temple School. As he has always said, "I was in charge for the first five minutes [of the 'Larry Mullen Band']. But as soon as Bono got there, I was out of a job."

28 As with Bono, the sudden death of Larry's mother was a tragic and pivotal moment in the life of the artist.

31 The Edge ranked 38th on the list of the 100 best guitar players of all time created by *Rolling Stone* magazine.

David Howell Evans, The Edge, was born August 8, 1961. He is not Irish; he was born in Barking, East London, to Garvin and Gwenda Evans, but he was only a year old when his parents decided to move to Dublin. He didn't go through any family tragedies or have any major problems as a teenager. Dave was a good kid, a good student, down-to-earth and sociable. He loved music and shared his interest with older brother Dick; they responded to Larry's band announcement together. His nickname, The Edge, was created by Bono, referring to his long face, but mostly because of his sharp intelligence.

> The Edge

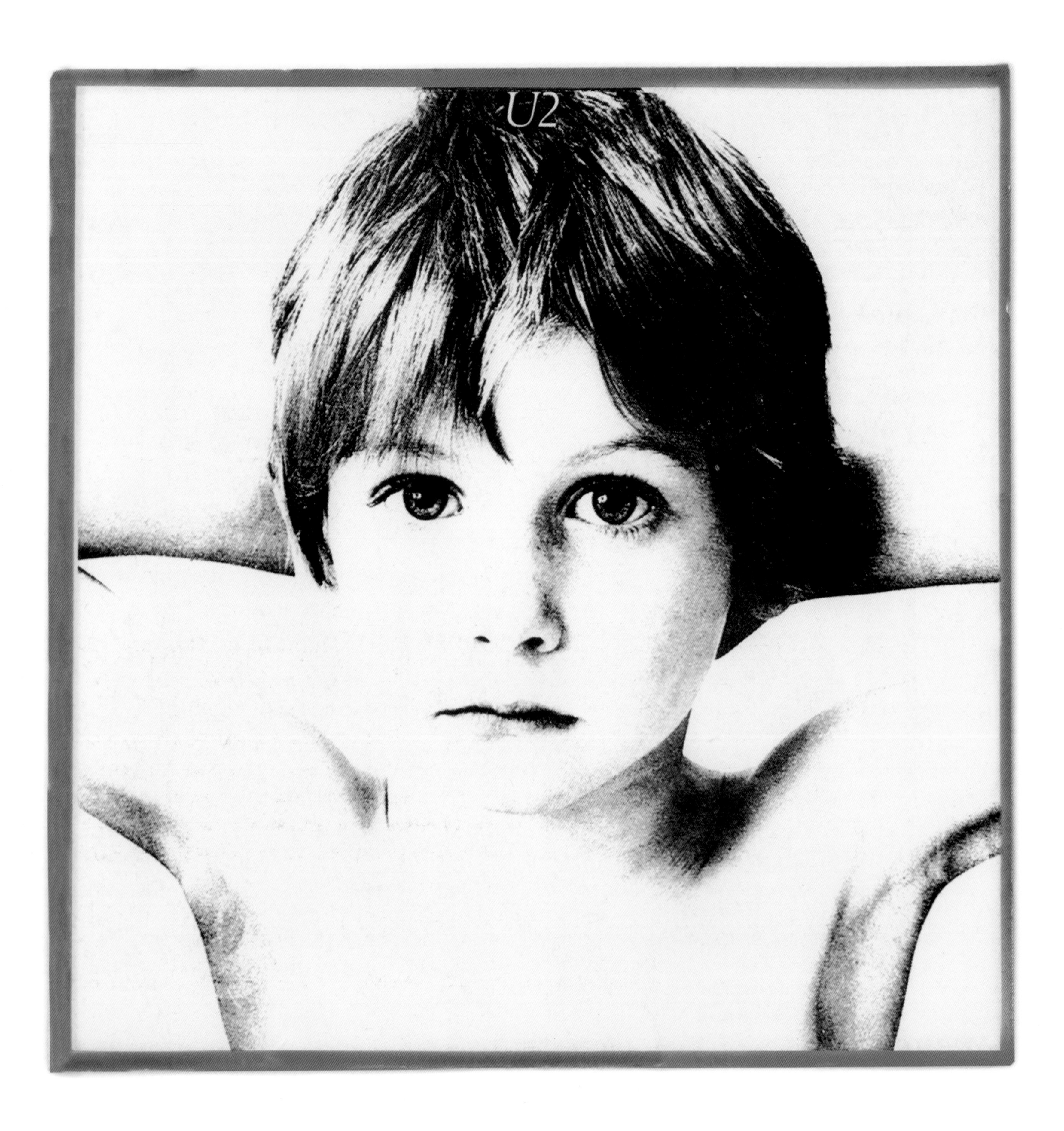
U2

But let's get back to the story. In March 1980, Chris Blackwell's Island Records signed U2, and the band went to work on its first album. Martin Hannett, who worked with them on "11 O'clock Tick Tock", was asked to produce it, but he declined because he was still reeling from the death of Joy Division's Ian Curtis. So, Steve Lillywhite became the producer and the band began to work with him at Windmill Lane Studios in Dublin. The band already had an established repertoire of about forty songs to choose from, but between March and September, they wrote and created new material. "It was a moment of great creativity and excitement," remembers Bono. "It seemed like everything we had dreamed about up until then was finally coming true. We wanted more from ourselves, our life, from the world and music, and to get it, we totally immersed ourselves in the studio work."

Boy was an almost perfect album, in terms of its construction, sound, and themes – the difficult transition from adolescence, pain, rage, sex and, love, with the exploration of powerful subjects and citations, from Oscar Wilde to William Golding. It was a "traditional" album for the time, which was in a complete post-punk tumult, the electronic revolution, and much more. But it was a truthful, honest, harsh and solid piece of work and, because of this, the public felt it and loved it. Bono knew exactly what he wanted. "I don't care about the obvious. Obviousness is like someone who says, 'let's be original.' Originality and change can come from different things than appearance. We're looking for those." And in fact, there was nothing superficial about *Boy*; but there was substance, feeling, passion, electric guitars, tight chords, and a voice – Bono's voice – that spoke to the listener's heart and mind.

U2 • BOY
CDCID 9646
I Will Follow
Twilight
An Cat Dubh
Into The Heart
Out Of Control
Stories For Boys
The Ocean
A Day Without Me
Another Time, Another Place
The Electric Co.
Shadows And Tall Trees
ISLAND

32 and 33 The boy on the cover of the album *Boy* is Peter Rowan, the brother of one of Bono's friends. He was also on the cover of *Three* and *War*. However, in the U.S., the album was released with a photo of the band members.

34 and 35 The band in a snow-covered playground. In December 1980, U2 played at El Mocambo in Toronto, Canada, in front of an audience of about eighty people.

36-37 The first international shows highlighted the band's great potential and the amazing charisma of its members.

WE PROMISED
HONESTY,
REBELLION,
STRENGTH,
MOVEMENT.

> Bono

U2 achieved some success and things changed, and while it was not a resounding success, it was enough to convince the band they were on the right track, to get more people to their concerts and give everyone hopes and dreams. In July 1981, they went into the studio to record their second album, again with Steve Lillywhite at Windmill Lane Studios. They worked hard for two months, even though they had a few problems, like the disappearance of Bono's suitcase, which had all the lyrics for the new songs, after a concert in Portland, Oregon. After all the doubts and difficulties, it took two months to bounce back and make a record in which spirituality dominated and rock ruled the dances, as perfectly demonstrated by the gripping single, destined to become one of the band's classics, "Gloria", or in songs like "Tomorrow" and "With a Shout." Were there any certainties? At that time, just when they had released a new album, had done a concert tour in Europe, had made a video for "Gloria" that found a huge fan base overseas, thanks to the launch of MTV, U2 was about to break up – and for religious reasons. It seemed inconceivable. Bono, The Edge and Larry Mullen participated in meetings for the Shalom Fellowship, a Christian congregation whose aim was to reconcile Catholics and Protestants, in the same period in which they began to write songs for their second album, *October*, from February 1981 until the end of the *Boy Tour*. The pressure on the band was intense and expectations from the record company and fans were high. But Larry, Bono and The Edge were not convinced that what they were doing was right. There was a contradiction in their new lives, which were made up of money, adoring fans, success, lights and color, and the lives of Christians who helped others, going to poorer or struggling countries. There was a contradiction in their faith and rock 'n' roll, or at least that was what their companions at the Shalom Fellowship claimed. Larry thought all this criticism was unjust and left the fellowship while The Edge didn't agree and decided to leave the band. He told Bono, who did the same. "I had to decide who to trust," remembers The Edge. "Were those, telling me that staying in the band was wrong, my friends? Or were my band mates, fans, and those who believed in what U2 did, right? I needed time to think about it," he said. "It's true, we were so close to breaking up," said Bono. "We were no longer sure we wanted to be a rock band. That world was shiny and vapid and we wanted something different." Then Bono realized that the solution was actually U2, to be your best self, to search for the good, and the opportunity to do great things; it was the reality of a band that could truly combine spirituality and electricity, hope and faith, rock and life.

39 The band began working on their second album, *October*, after the *Boy Tour*. They went into the studio in July 1981. The album has many references to faith and spirituality.

U2 OCTOBER

For him, the answer was God, not religion. He said, "Wherever I look I see the signs of a Creator. But I can't see it as a religion that has divided my people in two." And with that strength, and the examples of Patti Smith, Bob Dylan and many others, they were able to find balance between God and rock 'n' roll. U2 went forth and indeed took a giant and important step forward in their development.

October was a powerful and clear record that perfectly defined U2's world, their newfound balance and new strength. It was their second album, but it was already a step toward maturity. The crisis they had gone through allowed them to focus on their goals and their sound. Especially The Edge, who didn't do any of the things classic "guitar heroes" had always done, but contributed an original and innovative style to that perfect mix of tradition and modernity the band had in *October*.

40 and 40-41 U2 participated in the 12th Pinkpop Festival in Holland in 1981, performing to 50,000 people.

The year 1982 was mostly about concerts and meetings, like the one in February with photographer Anton Corbjin ("With U2, I always felt that Anton was photographing the songs, not us," said Bono), the early U.S. stadium dates, like opening for the J. Geils Band, and Bono and Ali's wedding in August. Then the band started working on a new album. But they were not the same U2 they had once been; they were no longer twenty year olds in love with rock, driven by the energy of punk rock music, anxious to ignite passion and enthusiasm in those who listened to it. They had been together for six years, had gone through personal and artistic growth, had questioned their faith and friendships, and had experienced the first glimmer of success together. *October* did well, but not amazingly well, and they had not yet earned a lot of money, but they were certain they could do more and better.

42-43 U2 played at the Gateshead Festival on July 31, 1981, opening for the Police. Bono stood out for his great energy and rapport with the audience.

43 Bono, who is graced with great acrobatic skills, at the US Festival in San Bernardino, California in 1983. The event was organized by Steve Wozniak, co-founder of Apple.

"More" and "better" happened with *War*, the third chapter of their musical adventure, or rather the final chapter of the first phase, the one of growth, a time when they were realizing their own talents and abilities, as well as who they were as a band and as themselves. For many, *War* could have had just one song, "Sunday Bloody Sunday", to deserve the success and attention it received at that point and going forward. The song was a passionate appeal for peace, recalling the killing of unarmed civilians by the British army in Northern Ireland in 1972. Bono simply said they wanted to be united and didn't want to sing songs like that anymore. It was a very difficult position to take in the middle of a war that had bloodied the streets of Northern Ireland for decades; it was a difficult position to take for a rock band. But it was a position U2 wanted to take, or rather had to take, to give meaning to their existence as a band. It was a song of peace and unity, it was "not a rebel song," as Bono had always said. It wasn't a call for more killing, or to push others to violence, revenge or a revolution. It was about peace, and at a concert, Bono raised his white flag to clarify that even further.

Bono perfectly explained the meaning of the song on a dramatic day, many years later during *The Joshua Tree Tour*. On November 8, 1987, the IRA, the armed Catholic group who fought against the British occupation of Northern Ireland, bombed the Unionist Protestants in Enniskillen during a Remembrance ceremony, a commemoration of British war victims. Eleven people, mostly elderly pensioners, died in the attack. That same day, during the performance of "Sunday Bloody Sunday" at a concert in Denver, Bono said, "And let me tell you something. I've had enough of Irish Americans, who haven't been back to their country in twenty or thirty years, come up to me and talk about the resistance, the revolution back home, and the glory of the revolution, and the glory of dying for the revolution. Fuck the revolution! They don't talk about the glory of killing for the revolution. What's the glory in taking a man from his bed and gunning him down in front of his wife and his children? Where's the glory in that? Where's the glory in bombing a Remembrance Day parade of old-age pensioners, their medals taken out and polished up for the day. Where's the glory in that? To leave them dying or crippled for life or dead under the rubble of the revolution, that the majority of the people in my country don't want. No more! Sing no more!"

There were more dreams, more desires for understanding, peace, and unity and many other songs on the record called *War*. U2 had found their mission – to try to make people think, touch their hearts, send a universal message and not take sides. "I don't want to talk about one side or the other, because conflict, any conflict, leaves hate and resentment in the hearts of men. And this is the war we have to fight, with ourselves, against hate and bitterness." And it was like that for the whole album. "Seconds" talked about the nuclear arms race and "New Year's Day" talked in some way about Solidarnosc (Independent Self-governing Trade Union "Solidarity") and what was going on in Poland. Their songs were meant to leave a mark, they were meant to endure.

The record was a success and, for the first time, U2 reached the top of the U.K. charts, surpassing even Michael Jackson's *Thriller*. But British critics didn't particularly like the album, saying it was too "conservative" and too "rock" at a time when British music had discovered the New Dandies and MTV. The most relevant magazine at the time was *The Face*, and image counted and style was everything. The album tour was successful, especially in the U.S. where the June 5, 1983 concert at the Red Rocks Amphitheatre in Colorado aired on MTV. It became a video cassette and brought the *Under a Blood Red Sky* EP to life.

45 *War* was the band's third album, the culmination of a period of growth. It made number one in the U.K.

46 Bono in 1983, with a white flag, a sign of peace, during the taping of *The Tube*, a British music series.

U2
WAR

WHERE'S THE
GLORY IN THAT?
NO MORE!
SING NO MORE!

> Bono

BonoAdamLarryTheEdgeBonoAdamLarryTheEdge
AdamLarryTheEdgeBonoAdamLarryTheEdgeBono
LarryTheEdgeBonoAdamLarryTheEdgeBonoAdam
TheEdgeBonoAdamLarryTheEdgeBonoAdamLarry
BonoAdamLarryTheEdgeBonoAdamLarryTheEdge
AdamLarryTheEdgeBonoAdamLarryTheEdgeBono

48 and 49 In the beginning, Bono won over the audience with his intense performance and rebellious air, which slowly turned into political and social commitment.

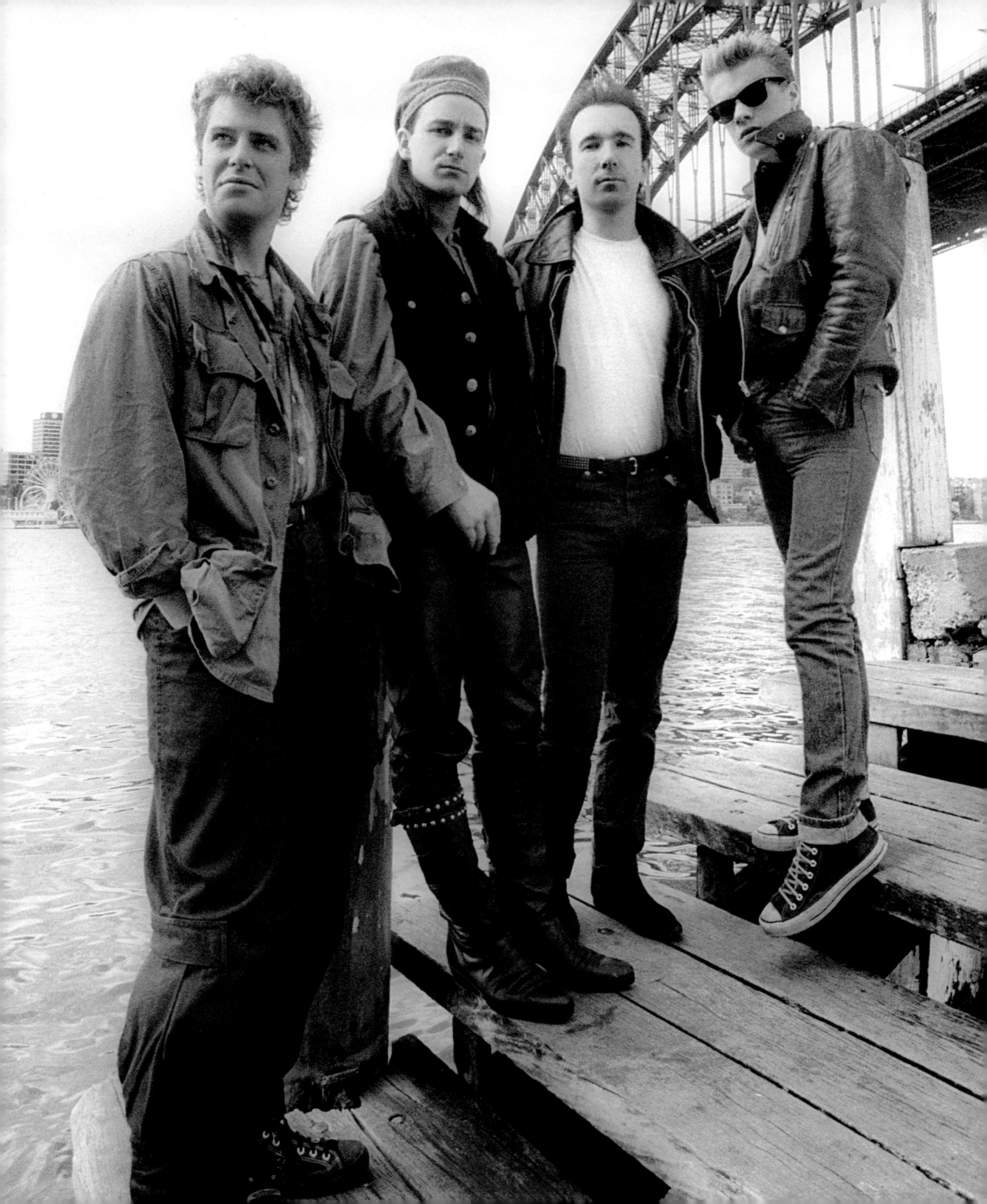

The Era
of Chang
CHAPTER TWO

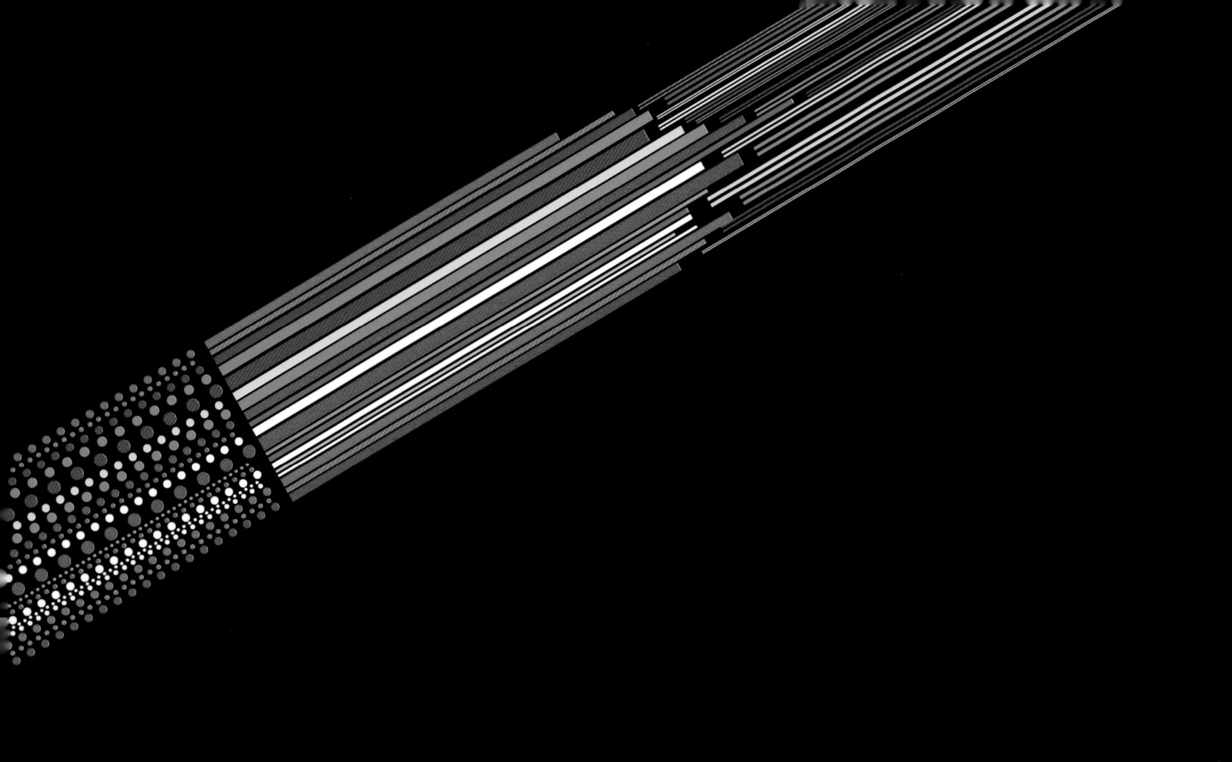

MY DESIRE TO EXPERIMENT
WAS ENORMOUS. THEY GAVE ME
TOTAL FREEDOM; I DIDN'T HAVE
TO SIMPLY KEEP THE TIME,
BUT I COULD FREE MY CREATIVITY
AND FIND INCREASINGLY BETTER
RESULTS.

> Larry

1984 was a year of change. There had been U2 before 1984 and there was U2 after 1984. And U2 was the one to make this change happen. The Edge remembers, "We didn't want to be the same. We didn't want to fall into the trap many bands fall into, where they let themselves be consumed by success, ride on it, have fun, fall apart, die, and leave nothing of themselves behind. For us, it was different. First of all, because U2's members were and are four friends. Our relationships go beyond the music, we are as close as a family and, at the same time, we are a working unit. This means that, like in a family, we grow and change together and that change and growth is reflected in the music we make. After *War*, our fan base clearly grew and they weren't the same ones from the beginning. We had the opportunity to speak to others, to show who we were to a larger audience. And we were much more than we had shown them up until then." To make this change, to show the world what they were able to do, they turned to Brian Eno to produce their next album. "We knew Eno's work and we were interested in it. We liked what he did with Talking Heads and most of all, his solo record, *Before and After Science.* We were already thinking about Eno's work when we were working on *War* with Steve Lillywhite."

"I got a phone call from Bono, who asked me to work with them. At the time, I had stopped producing records, plus I had lost all interest in rock; I was working with Daniel Lanois on projects that were far different, musically, from U2's music. But Bono was interesting, what he said was interesting, and the idea of our music interested him. I tried to warn him. I told him the final result would be very different from U2's prior records, that it would be almost unrecognizable and people might not understand. It didn't scare him. He said they didn't want to do the same thing, they didn't want to do what they had already done and they wanted to be different. I only asked to work with Daniel Lanois. They accepted and everything took off," remembered Brian Eno. The relationship with Brian Eno was paramount. Eno arrived with the conviction that rock no longer had anything to offer and that as a genre, it was dead, as a language it was on its last legs, and as a system of values it was history. Rock didn't interest him; it wasn't part of his world. But it only took one meeting with Bono in Dublin, a long lunch with the band, to make him understand they had infinite opportunities before them and that they could still involve rock.

Rock was facing its umpteenth death and U2 wanted to bring it back to life, they wanted to save it. In the mid-1980s, not only did new wave electronica take over the world, but pop was in full bloom. It seemed like rock was stuck in its own conventions and sounds, hindered by its complacencies; it was like a world standing still, incapable of moving forward. It wasn't like that for U2, and *The Unforgettable Fire* proved this without a shadow of a doubt. The band, their music, and that perfect formula, for which "three chords and the truth" were enough, had reached its peak. Perhaps it couldn't go any further.

The two 1983 albums, *War* and *Under a Blood Red Sky* had amply demonstrated that the band was ready to conquer the world. But for U2, that was all a waste without taking a step forward, without doing something that would push them into that "intellectual" elite group that they were not a part of. They didn't want to limit themselves to a rock sound; they wanted to change rock, they wanted to save rock. And they did it.

The Unforgettable Fire is an extraordinary album, in the literal sense of the word. There is very little of the ordinary. There is nothing ordinary about the use of rhythm, due partly to Eno's rhythmic composition but more to Larry Mullen's desire to push himself beyond his limits, "My technical abilities were limited, but my desire to experiment was enormous. Eno and Lanois gave me total freedom; I didn't have to simply keep the time, but I could free my creativity and find increasingly better results along with them." And the same thing happened with The Edge and his guitar. He found his absolute and innovative essence with Eno and Lanois. It was absolutely fundamental that The Edge's sound – which was already original – was convincing and unique in a time that was dominated by electronic keyboards and when the sound of the guitar immediately associated those who used one with a hypothetical distant past of rock. For Eno, who grew up in the cult of the visionary guitar playing of Robert Fripp, working with The Edge became the focus, contributing largely to the new sound of U2, without betraying the past. It is true that *The Unforgettable Fire* put U2 in a new category, but it is also true that their past work was not forgotten. The band's approach was about an incredible and immediate truth, nothing was unnatural or fake, nothing was random or lacking motive. Rock was part of it; and it was all there, strong and passionate. But, at the same time, the band went in a completely different direction. A new wave with body and soul and in fact, it led them to success, make no mistake. "Eno was looking for something new everywhere and he got bored with the same old, traditional songs. But Daniel Lanois was there for that and the balance was perfect," remembers Bono.

The release of *The Unforgettable Fire* was sensational and surprising, it unexpectedly brought together old rockers and young new wavers; rock enthusiasts could, once again, find themselves in one band all at once. And that is how it went. It was immediately obvious in the concerts following the release of the album. The youth, of the mid-1980s particularly, loved U2, because their music was full of tension, hope and atmosphere, which had disappeared at the end of the punk era, or perhaps even before.

50 1984, the beginning of their collaboration with Brian Eno. It was a turning point that opened the door to worldwide recognition.

55 Moydrum Castle, Athlone, County Westmeath, Ireland. From the cover of *The Unforgettable Fire*.

U2 The Unforgettable Fire

They were a passionate, warm and communicative band, committed to a social battle that was not a cliché. At the same time, they were anxious to find a new musical dimension for 1980s rock. Because we are talking about rock, in the most traditional sense, with guitars and not synthesizers, and sweat, tears and a few, simple chords that magically expressed the feelings of the changing times. When they played live, they were able to confirm, without a shadow of a doubt, that they held the key to the rock of the times, with a simple and intelligent synthesis of the past and the present (Irish tradition and rock 'n' roll, re-interpreted with an absolute contemporary sensibility), and that they were able to speak to the audience without any mediation. The most important thing was that the sound mix created with Brian Eno and Daniel Lanois was not lost in live concerts. U2 played with a fresh new sound and there was no manipulation or fakery; the transformation of the band was complete. Throughout everything, Bono was armed with a powerful and individual voice and a humble presence that was void of any rock star behavior. He was in control yet full of energy. He would invite the audience to sing, bring a girl from the front row on stage, give her a long hug, and say thanks countless times; he'd apologize to those who couldn't get in, and was natural, making friendly gestures like opening a bottle of wine and handing out glasses to those crowded around the stage. It was an unusual kindness for rock concerts at a time when it was more likely to go to blows with security than communicate with those on stage. It was the dream of rock 'n' roll, which was back for those who still wanted to experience it. It was the dream of eternal youth, experienced with a guitar in hand, singing, just like the title of U2's famous album *Under a Blood Red Sky*.

56-57 *The Unforgettable Fire Tour* began in New Zealand and Australia. U2 performed in 113 cities.

Live Aid sealed the deal the following year. The mega-concert, organized by Bob Geldof to shake up universal public opinion about world hunger, marked the beginning of a new era for U2. When, during a live broadcast, Bono broke the show rules and climbed over the police, security guards and barricades to hug a girl (two, to be exact) in the audience, it was an historic gesture on his part. By insisting, pushing aside bodyguards and police, he disregarded big concert rituals to do what he did at all U2 concerts, which was to eliminate the distance between the audience and the stage. It was not with the spirit of the rebellious punk era, but with the collective spirit of classic rock. Bono and his audience are one, and they must be one. Live Aid was proof that a rock audience could still be one, totally united. The hug was an extraordinary moment, one that Bono repeated at many concerts and that helped U2 go to the next level in terms of worldwide fame as well as in their understanding of the world. They were on the right track, one that would unite the old and the new, the past and the future. Rock as it was and what it had the potential to be. Everything changed after that concert because if the world and rock were changing, U2 was ahead of the game. Even more than Springsteen, who tried to escape tradition with *Born in the USA*, or David Bowie, who tried to renew himself with *Let's Dance* or new wave bands that flirted with electronica. U2 became the best, and certainly the most loved "reformers" of 1980s rock. With great intelligence, Bono, Adam Clayton, The Edge, and Larry Mullen Jr. slowly rebuilt the fabric of a rock culture that, in its thirty-year history, had worn many different hats and frequented different ideals and movements. It was animated by

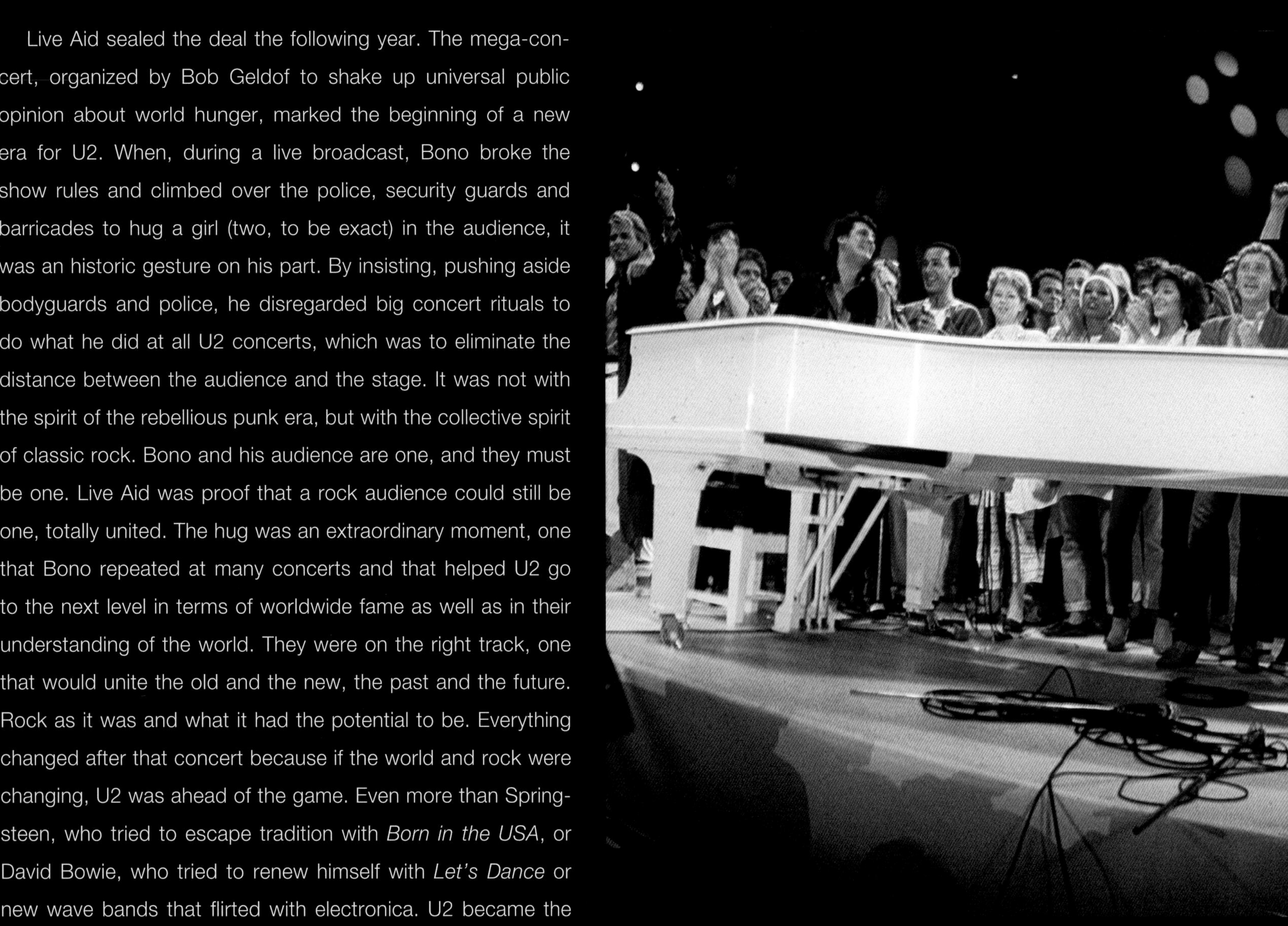

dreams and sounds that had often been contradictory, succeeding in always being the language of reality, the voice of youth, and a driving consciousness in a time that was moving rapidly, and constantly changing, again and again.

58-59 U2 were members of rock's elite, as seen in this 1985 Live Aid photo. Bono is center stage with Paul McCartney and George Michael.

1984-1989

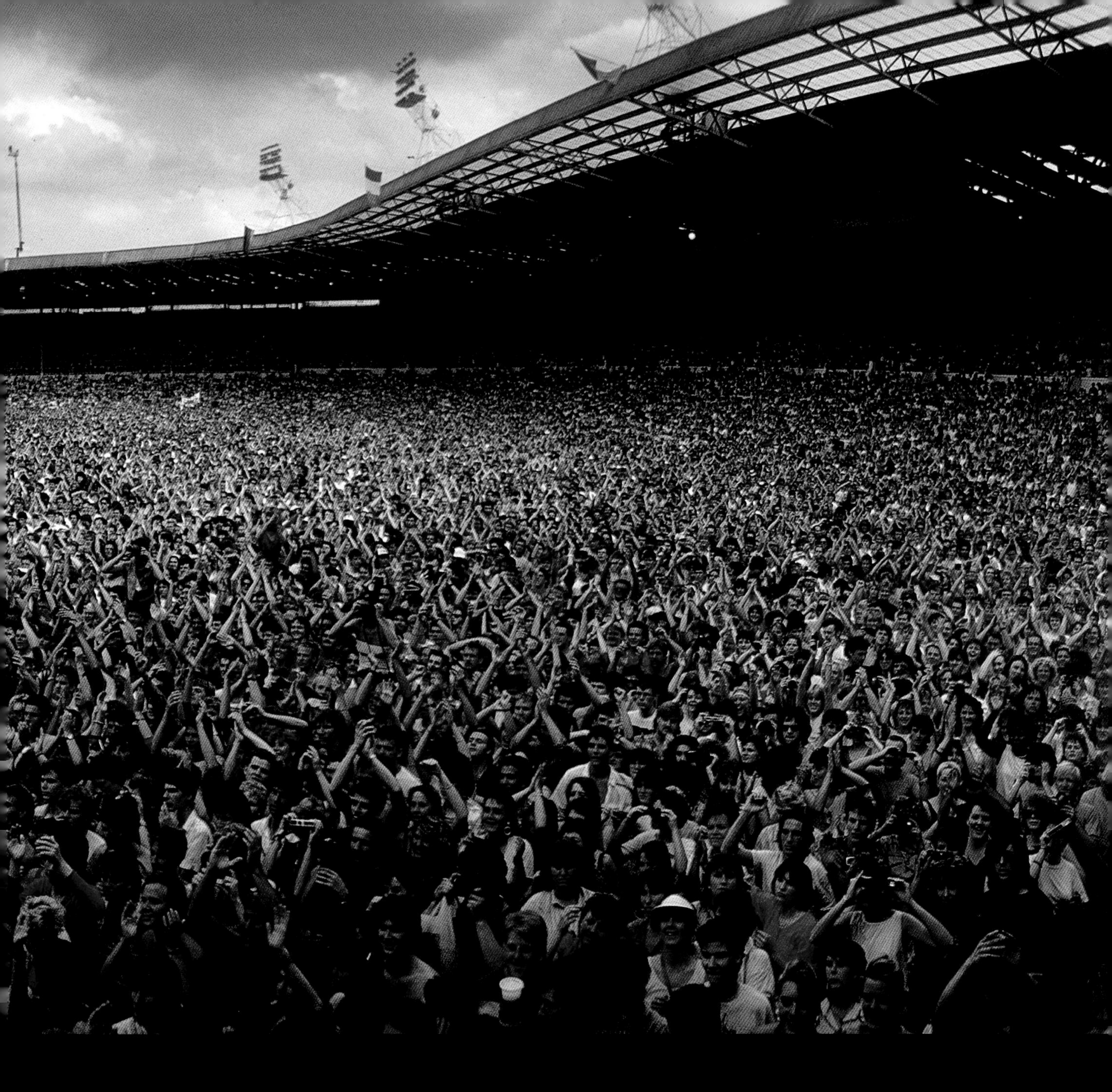

60-61 A huge audience at Live Aid in 1985, at Wembley Stadium. The engaging and intense performance rein

62 Bono's great physical exertion manifested in moments of exhaustion.

63 U2 had three songs on the line-up for Live Aid. They planned to play "Sunday Bloody Sunday", "Bad" and "Pride", but could only play the first two because of time constraints.

The Joshua Tree, the band's next album, released in 1986, succinctly and effectively interpreted the changes that were happening; it wasn't just about the dream of a perpetually young, free and defiant rock as much as the need for purity, peace and innocence of a generation that was timidly trying to create new idols and new ideals for themselves. *The Joshua Tree* was exemplary in this sense. The themes dealt with a desperate search for identity, like when Bono sang "I Still Haven't Found What I'm Looking for" in an emotionally involved and well-constructed piece; or the fight for life in a difficult situation in "Running to Stand Still"; the vivid portrait of a small mining town and the condemnation of the humiliation miners faced in "Red Hill Mining Town"; the profoundly deep song "One Tree Hill", an ultra-modern gospel played by the band in a crescendo of remarkable tension; the beautiful "Exit"; or the last song, "Mothers of the Disappeared", a tribute to Amnesty International, which U2 supported on many occasions. Bono's and the band's experience working with Amnesty International in 1986 for the *Conspiracy of Hope Tour* was crucial for them. They visited Nicaragua and El Salvador and saw suffering in many parts of the world. They stood against indifference alongside many other big names in rock, and found yet another reason for being, as a band, as rock artists, and as human beings. The songs on *The Joshua Tree* album are the perfect reflection of all this. While the lyrics Bono wrote were beautiful and important, the music on this record was totally solid, rich and captivating. And, by their own admission, *The Unforgettable Fire* was an "incomplete" or unfinished work or conversation. But, *The Joshua Tree*, through the strength of the band's rock style, had completely fused with the refined musical sensibility of Brian Eno and Daniel Lanois, who were the producers once again, enriching the band's sound, with unexpected openings, combining different emotions and feelings. *The Joshua Tree* had all the strength of new wave, the energy of tradition, the love of experimentation, and loyalty to the times. This meant going from moments when U2 could have been the Doors or Pink Floyd, like in "Bullet The Blue Sky", to slow acoustic ballads, to the search for a unique language for an all-encompassing and multi-faceted rock, like that of today. With *The Joshua Tree*, U2 joined a different league, the greatest in rock 'n' roll. This was all followed by successful tours, being mobbed by fans, chart-topping hits all over the world, and much more. Bono became the "messiah" of rock, with his pronounced spirituality, and demonstrated social and political commitment, temperate power, and an ability to transform shouts into prayers, a whisper into a sharp blade. "For me, it's as if it was our second album.

65 *The Joshua Tree* owes its name to a typical plant from the southwestern U.S. The album won a Grammy Award in 1988 for Album of the Year.

U 2
T H E
J O S H U A
T R E E

The first was *The Unforgettable Fire*," said Bono. And perhaps he was right, because the intellectual, creative, sentimental, and musical change from their first three and the last two releases were immeasurable. And everything that was still in development in their first three albums, found complete realization in the later two, in which U2 gave meaning to their name, creating a single global community of their fans, and truly becoming the band they wanted to be. The tour was enormous, in every sense of the word, in terms of the sound, the emotional impact, the creative freedom, and in the relationships with the audiences. At the time, Bono said, "What makes us keep going on a tour this big is really the enthusiasm of the people. As long as the people are with us, everything goes well. You can use the rhythm of the street, and best use your energy. But you can't do it with that alone. It's the energy of the audience, every night, that pushes you forward. If my voice is cracking, there's an audience every night that sings with me and helps me." U2 has a tight relationship with its fans, a trusted and affectionate relationship that seems to be truly unique in the world of rock. "We feel very close to our fans because we were just like them. When we became a band in the late 1970s, we went to see The Clash when they were playing in Dublin; we experienced the music we listened to. We were like our fans, and now we are on the stage, and that is the only difference between us." Perhaps it was not the only one, given the great success U2 has enjoyed the world over, a success that, without doubt, brought the foursome incredible earnings. "It's true, rock pays their stars too much, but none of us got involved in rock to make money or to get rich. The problem of money is one that we've never faced as a band and I don't know how much trouble it could bring us. But it is also great having a lot of money, to help our families and friends and to enjoy the fruits of our work. And then I think our country, with the taxes, has earned a lot more from us than we have now." U2's country is Ireland, a beautiful and troubled country, with which it has a loving relationship, free from any cliché, devoid of any kind of nationalism. And even though they were trailblazers, they always remained deeply attached to their roots, to Ireland, a land that is not just about jigs, reels, and traditional music, but also a land of great rock. "The Irish built America," said The Edge, explaining the bridge the band is crossing, and has crossed. "I didn't have a way to understand my Irishness until we went to America and we discovered the nature and strength, but also the alienation," he said. Bono echoed this, "I didn't know I was Irish until I went to America. When we cut *Boy*, we went to America for the first time and everyone asked what it was like living in Ireland, what we thought of the political and religious conflict in our country and the problems with England. It was then that we really began to think about what had happened before our eyes up until then and we wrote songs like 'Sunday Bloody Sunday'." You have to be outside of a situation to really see it." U2 is the only band, today, that still knows how to combine the urgency of new wave with the tradition and fervor of rock and the roots of the blues. "We didn't care just about the blues, but about all kinds of popular music. With blues though, we had a unique relationship. When we got together as a band, we were part of the punk rock explosion of 1976 and we rejected everything there was before it. Today we are a different band, in search of the music of the roots, those that gave rock 'n' roll its start," explained The Edge. "It was the spirit of the blues that interested us, not necessarily the form. If you listen to blues or gospel music, you discover an incredible sense of abandon, freedom, space, while on the other side, modern music is tight and claustrophobic; it wasn't freeing, it hid behind a trend or an image. But the spirit of true rock 'n' roll was one of abandon and this was the one that was always rejected by a majority of the audience, the conformists.

67 Once again on stage at Wembley Stadium in London. Bono and The Edge during a concert for *The Joshua Tree Tour*, in June 1987.

1984-1989

68-69 *The Joshua Tree Tour* was a great success. They had 112 sell-out dates.

AIRC BIRKHOFF
RIKXOORT

Today, there is a new sense of conservatism, especially in music; there is a new claustrophobia, rock 'n' roll has been vested with a jacket that's too tight, while many bands are trying to break rock out of this cage," added Bono. Famous, strong and passionate, U2 became the symbol of a more dynamic rock, more active in terms of civil rights, social battles, and not just with their songs, but also by offering concrete support to Amnesty International. "We reached a point where we felt we needed to do something, because we were in a position to use a lot of opportunities and it would have been stupid not to. I think that the future for us and for rock is to commit to smaller more direct and immediate objectives in addition to the big battles, like Live Aid or Amnesty. We aren't leaders, we are normal people who were inspired by music and hope that their music can inspire others to do something. We don't like the idea people have that U2 wants to carry the weight of the world's problems on their shoulders, we wouldn't be able to bear such a responsibility. I hate the idea that rock stars are supposed to be leaders of their generation, what a ridiculous idea. It is sad that people are so disappointed by politicians and politics that they need to put rock stars on a social pedestal. We don't consider ourselves rock stars, let alone politicians," said Bono.

70 U2 were inspired by American music, like country and the blues on *The Joshua Tree*. Part of the album was recorded at Sun Studio in Memphis.

71 Rock commitment and social activism: U2's direction was clear at this time. With *The Joshua Tree*, even the band's sound was established.

I DIDN'T HAVE
A WAY TO
UNDERSTAND
MY IRISHNESS
UNTIL WE WENT
TO AMERICA.

> The Edge

WHAT MAKES US
KEEP GOING ON
A TOUR THIS BIG
IS REALLY THE
ENTHUSIASM
OF THE PEOPLE.

> Bono

I LIKED THE IDEA
OF MAKING SOME
NOISE WITH
THE OTHERS.
I DIDN'T HAVE
ANY PARTICULAR
EXPECTATIONS;
WE WANTED
TO HAVE FUN.

> Larry

FOR US THERE'S
U2 MUSIC, AND
THEN THERE'S
EVERYTHING ELSE.

> Adam

IT'S THE ENERGY
OF THE AUDIENCE,
EVERY NIGHT,
THAT PUSHES
YOU FORWARD.
IF MY VOICE IS
CRACKING, THERE'S
AN AUDIENCE
EVERY NIGHT THAT
SINGS WITH ME
AND HELPS ME.

> Bono

80-81 A moment of relaxation for the band between rehearsals for the numerous concerts played in 1987-88.

U2's mistake, their first "wrong" move, came in 1987, with tremendous force in the form of a biography called *Unforgettable Fire*, by Eamon Dunphy, the double album *Rattle and Hum*, and finally a rockumentary of the same name, which premiered worldwide on October 27, 1987 in Dublin. As for the book, which promised to be the best-selling biography of all time, it was already controversial. *Rattle and Hum* was rather unusual in comparison to market stereotypes in that it was a double album that had both new songs, recorded in the studio, and live songs, from the previous year's tour. It was a sort of "snapshot" of the band as well as an album in which the band's acclaimed "honesty" seemed to change into boastfulness for the first time. It was not so much because of the album, which, in reality, allowed fans to listen to both key aspects of U2's personality – the stylistic consistency of their new compositions as well as the untamable emotional fire of their concerts – supported by an historical perspective woven through the work, which was the desire to offer the public a precise awareness of the history of rock. One need only consider the opening track, a vibrant live version of "Helter Skelter", an ode to pandemonium, to uncontrolled chaos, one of the last songs by the Beatles. But, it also includes Bob Dylan's "All Along the Watchtower", Hendrix and his guitar as he shreds the "Star-Spangled Banner", "God Part II", dedicated to John Lennon and "Angel of Harlem", dedicated to Billie Holiday. And that was not all. There was also a piece written by and sung with Bob Dylan, and one where you hear the voice and guitar of B.B. King, a gospel choir, and even two street musicians. It seemed like a small mosaic in which the pieces were precisely chosen with the intention of creating an indispensable summary, citing the basic fundamentals of rock culture, from U2's point of view, naturally. Essentially, the album had all the explosive passion of rock, embodied by the band in those years. It also seemed to be a major rock apotheosis, closing a cycle that began just three years earlier, when the American magazine, *Rolling Stone* named them "the" band of the 1980s.

Everything was "huge", self-affirming, highly pompous, and extravagant; it was a sort of repositioning of the band among the greatest in rock, but done by themselves, with a touch of arrogance. That arrogance became even clearer in the film directed by Phil Joanou. In it, they were a little more self-congratulatory than necessary and their propensity to be missionaries of new teachings, messengers that spoke of energy and spirituality, was, perhaps, magnified beyond any self-imposed reasonable limit.

83 The title of the album *Rattle and Hum*, was inspired by a verse in the song "Bullet The Blue Sky" on *The Joshua Tree*.

84-85 The *Rattle and Hum* documentary was released in Ireland in October 1988 and in the U.S. that November.

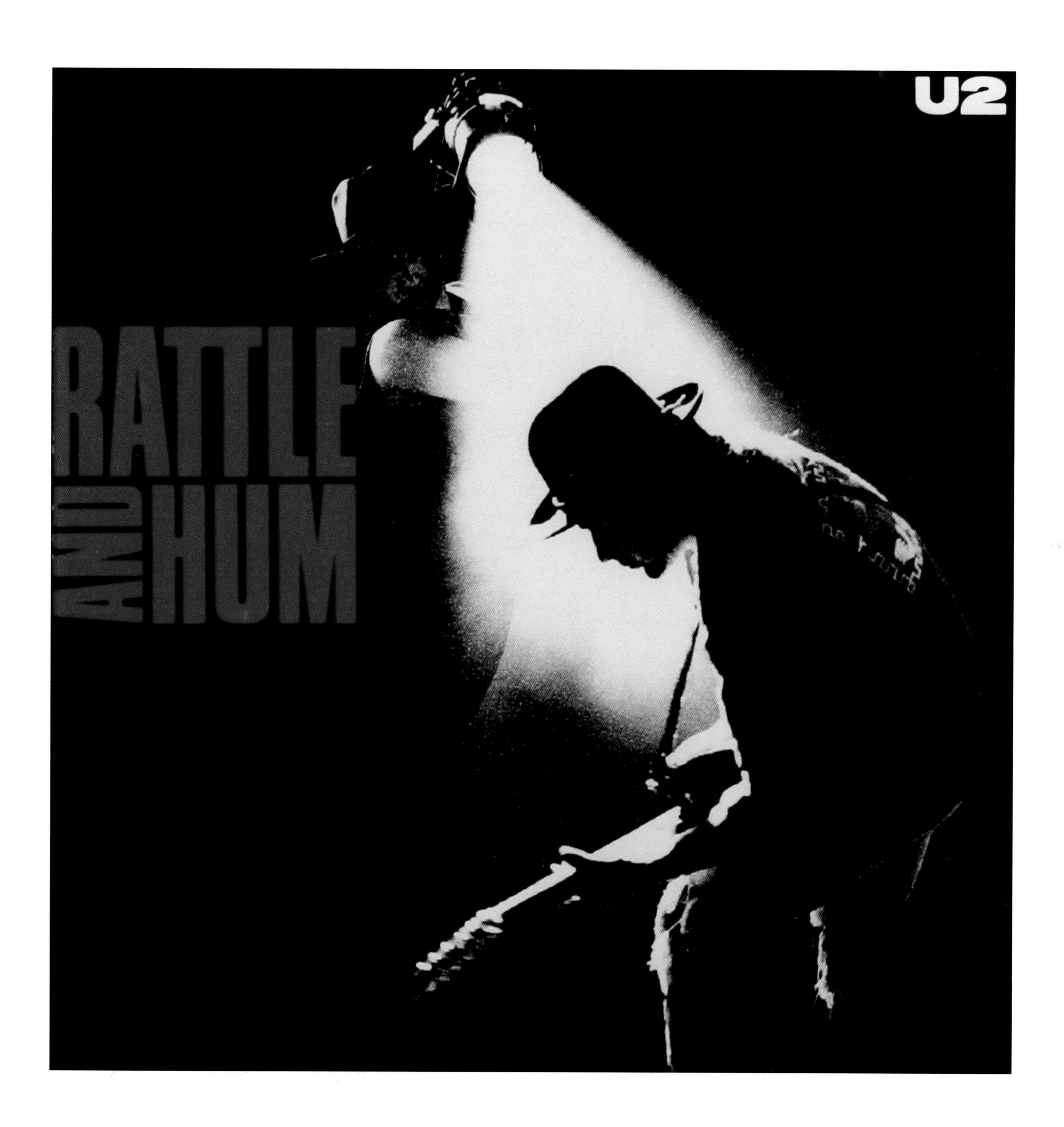
U2
RATTLE
AND
HUM

U2
RATTLE AND HUM
THE MOVIE

WHEN WE GO IN THE STUDIO TO RECORD, WE'RE MORE LIKE ARTISTS; WE DON'T KNOW WHAT'S GOING TO HAPPEN. WHEN WE GO ON STAGE, WE'RE MORE ENTERTAINERS.

> Adam

1984-1989

86-87 Bono signs autographs for fans. *The Joshua Tree* further increased the band's fan base.

87 Adam signs promotional materials for the release of *Rattle and Hum*. It topped the album charts in many countries.

Thus, the trip to the U.S. marked a new turning point, because U2 needed to search for their musical roots, to envelop themselves in the blues, soul, and the kind of rock that contributed to carving out their universal sound and culture. They needed to discover America, the infinite, immense, and profound America and to find poetry and pain, magic and mystery, joy and chaos. They needed to get out of their world and discover another. Their motivations were correct, but at the same time, the band lost control of itself and exaggerated things. They exceeded the limits of their traditional restraint. To put it simply, they got big headed. It got to the point where *The New York Times* reviewed the record and the film and wrote that it was an exercise in "pure egomania." Now, since the dust has settled, many have revisited and re-listened to the *Rattle and Hum* "chapter" (intentionally realized without the Eno/Lanois team in favor of Jimmy Iovine, a classic rock producer), without considering the relationship with the film – which perhaps is fair – and focusing on the album, which, in reality, has many gems and is essential to understanding the band's subsequent moves. *Rattle and Hum* was, perhaps, a necessary stop on a journey that could never end, in which their discomfort with everything that is acquired – certainty, dogma and stagnation – became manifest once again. When they went back on tour the following year, they were still fantastic and unbeatable in terms of their energy on stage, but they were definitely at a pivotal crossroads for basic choices. They peaked with *The Joshua Tree*; it was the best and purest expression of their poetry. Then with *Rattle and Hum*, they went back on the road, looking for new territories and a meeting, but not a revivalist one. They wanted to walk rock's journey, with its black roots and its big names like Dylan, Lennon and Hendrix. They say it themselves in "God Part II", one of the most exciting parts of the concert. Bono was on the edge of the stage, vested as a special preacher of messages of love and he sang, "Don't believe in the '60s, the golden age of pop" and even before that, "Don't believe that rock 'n' roll can really change the world". What was painfully clear was that U2 was, once again, ready to turn the page.

88 and 89 Historic meetings: two of the best guitar players, The Edge and Keith Richards, together on stage for a benefit concert (left) and Bono in a performance with Bob Dylan.

90 Bono at the Nassau Coliseum in Uniondale, New York, during *The Joshua Tree Tour.*

91 Video of many *Joshua Tree Tour* dates was added to the 1988 *Rattle and Hum* documentary.

92-93 Blues roots: Bono in concert with B.B. King during the *Love Town Tour*, 47 dates in 1989-90.

94 and 95 Two shots of the band taken to promote their albums in the late 1980s. The photo on the left was taken on the roof of the Million Dollar Hotel in Los Angeles, which is shown in the video "Where the Streets Have No Name", and is the protagonist of the film of the same name by Wim Wenders in 2000, whose soundtrack was written by Bono.

1984-1989

NDD • Issue 489 • November 1993 $3.95 $NZ 5.50 (GST

Ro Stone

You Am I
Breeders
Iggy Pop
Crowded House
The Fall
Evan Dando

The Edge Takes Charge

Soul Asylun

Platinum Punks

Countdow The Glan Years

Yothu Yindi's

Velvet Revolution

Bullets & Ballot

Australia's Extreme Right

U2's Zoo World Order

Win a Walkman

ISSN 1320-0615
771320 061002

U

Reinvention and the Conquest of Creative Freedom

CHAPTER THREE

2

WE DIDN'T WANT TO BE THE SAME.
WE DIDN'T WANT TO FALL INTO THE
TRAP MANY BANDS FALL INTO, WHERE
THEY LET THEMSELVES BE CONSUMED
BY SUCCESS, RIDE ON IT, HAVE
FUN, FALL APART, DIE, AND LEAVE
NOTHING OF THEMSELVES BEHIND.
FOR US, IT WAS DIFFERENT. FIRST
OF ALL, BECAUSE U2'S MEMBERS
WERE AND ARE FOUR FRIENDS.
OUR RELATIONSHIPS GO BEYOND
THE MUSIC, WE ARE AS CLOSE
AS A FAMILY AND, AT THE SAME
TIME, WE ARE A WORKING UNIT.

> The Edge

The change took them to Berlin in October of 1990, to start a new album at Hansa Studios, with Eno and Lanois, in a city that was still seething from the Fall of the Wall, where life, the past, death and the future seemed to perfectly co-exist. For the first time, the four band members experienced the turning point differently. They clashed and argued constantly about the direction they should take while they were working on the album because Mullen and Clayton wanted to go back to the sound of their previous two releases while The Edge and Bono wanted a radical change, inspired by electronica, independent rock, and dance music. This fracture seemed almost to push the band toward breaking up. "Larry and Adam weren't really satisfied with our sound; they didn't want it and we accused them of just wanting to be rock stars. Maybe they were right. They pointed their finger at the fact that we didn't have songs, The Edge and I wanted to concentrate on the sound and we couldn't see outside of that. But at the same time, they could have pushed us to be better and encouraged us, instead of accusing us," said Bono. "Maybe we were wrong in rushing things and going straight to Berlin. We could have worked in Dublin, with no pressure, and focused better on things. The fact is, I was listening to other things, like the Nine Inch Nails, the Stone Roses, New Order, and Einzurstende Neubauten," added The Edge. As often happens, the magic of the moment resolved everything, putting everything on the right track. It happened when the band, almost improvising, found a masterpiece like "One" in their hands. The spark was re-ignited and the four understood each other once again and their work finally began to take shape.

Achtung Baby came out in November 1991 and left many of U2's fans dumbfounded because it largely left behind the classic, epic and romantic sound that marked some of their best music, choosing a new and genuinely original fusion of different elements, from the psychedelia of the latest American stars to dance music beats, which branded the music of many English bands (from the Stone Roses to Happy Mondays), culminating in electronica and "noise", the exaggerated use of distortion and guitar feedback that dominated almost the whole album. Hence, it was a step forward, a determined attempt to clean up any confusion following the release of *Rattle and Hum* and to head straight for a major sound and emotional renewal. It was both an easy and difficult album. It was easy because many of the songs were captivating, full of catchy melodies, rhythmic and even danceable (in reality, it was a tendency U2 always had). It was difficult because aside from the structure of the songs, which were often exceptionally simple, the album was extremely elaborate in terms of its sounds. In addition to Brian Eno and Daniel Lanois, five other people, including Steve Lillywhite, worked on the production, sound mix, and engineering. That was what made this album so original, a modern and stylistic gem. One could tell from the beginning that it had a different sound from the others, even from the opening track, "Zoo Station", which was unbelievably styled by the production team, even distorting Bono's voice using filters. The song is haunting, which immediately states the bands intentions. But the other songs on the album are no less explosive or engaging, from "Even Better Than the Real Thing", Manchester-like and highly enjoyable, to "One", a ballad where Bono's voice rules, and the song that was part of the new film by Wim Wenders, "Until the End of the World", which was more in line with U2's classic style. More than Bono's voice, The Edge's guitar marked the exciting passages on this album, as with "Who's Gonna Ride Your Wild Horses", a perfect hit single with a catchy refrain, a song of love and passion that highlights the pop talents of the band. But, it is The Edge's work, which is noisy and bare, where the band found an unexpected element of change. Other songs must be mentioned like "So Cruel", one of the best tracks on the album, with its gospel air and minimalist violins, a gem of fusion and creativity, as well as the most charismatic and easiest of songs, "Mysterious Ways" and the last songs, "Acrobat", the only song to touch on the politics and religion of the band, and "Love is Blindness", a sort of heart-wrenching and mysterious blues song. Finally, it was no coincidence that on the album cover, the band gave special thanks to the likes of David Bowie, Peter Gabriel and Lou Reed who, along with Eno, permanently bound U2's musical journey to the best creative teachings of British rock. Nor was it a coincidence that part of this album was made in Berlin, given the atmosphere that dominated it, where light and dark often met, and passion and energy became a lyrical language, an elusive melody, the greatest rock of all. The album marked a new and radical departure from what the band had done up until that time. It was a new breaking point, a step forward. And the public, accustomed to seeing U2 as cutting-edge in conceptual innovation in rock, followed them. Or rather, it carried them to victory because the album was hugely successful, with five singles on the charts, including "The Fly", "Mysterious Ways" and obviously the very beautiful, "One". But U2 was not satisfied. If the music changed, then the shows had to change, or rather, they had to become multi-media performances perfectly in line with the changes in the world, which between satellites and the Internet truly began to be the global village envisioned by Marshall McLuhan.

96 The October 14, 1993 cover of *Rolling Stone* was dedicated to The Edge and to the release U2's *Zooropa* album.

101 Perhaps no city other than Berlin, could have inspired the music heard on *Achtung Baby* in 1991.

As for the rest, Bono had clear ideas and said, "Rock has to be at the center of contradictions." And the *Zoo TV Tour*, U2's first in five years, which started in Lakeland, Florida on February 29, 1992, was definitely at the center of contradictions of early-1990s rock. The show was completely different from anything rock had ever offered, based on musical and visual chaos, symbolized by the phrase dominating the dozen or so screens that filled the stage as well as the concert tickets: "Everything you know is wrong". More than a stage, U2 proposed a multimedia installation, designed by Willie Williams in collaboration with Mark Fisher and Jonathan Park, with Brian Eno's vital help. The main part of the stage was about 250 feet (75 meters) wide and 80 feet (25 meters) high, with four large screens, 36 monitors, and 11 cars suspended in the air. A rich and complex show, it opened with a Trabant, an East German icon, which descended from the ceiling. It was rigged as a DJ booth and blared a "soundtrack" including Led Zeppelin, Nirvana, Bob Marley and The Waterboys, before the band arrived. And when the band did arrive, it was clear, the past was behind them. The tight and electric sounds of *Achtung Baby*, their latest album, dominated the entire night, from the opening songs "Zoo Station" and "The Fly" to the show's close in total darkness with "Love is Blindness". But the show was also full of irony and surprises. The beginning was electrifying, noisy, and chaotic and U2 was at the center of a universe full of information and messages "shouted" from dozens of "Zoo TV" televisions, with a video installation that was connected to a satellite dish. Video clips, random broadcasting excerpts, and images from the concert quickly and exasperatedly alternated, with flashing texts like, "Call your mother", "Watch more television", "It's your world, and you can change it", along with words, signs and video noise that blended in with the sounds on the stage, turning the concert into a high-impact psychedelic carnival. There were few stage lights, most of the lighting came from the television screens at the beginning of the concert. It was like a constant flicker of black and white that magnificently fused with the simplicity of a show that set aside the epic spirit the band had accustomed us to in the past to redirect everything towards an exasperated physicality, a burning realism. It was all about visionary technology and electronic psychedelia – to put it simply, it was rock for a band that had changed, and was no longer "messianic"; one that no longer had certainties and, in fact, wanted to share their doubts with the public. So much so, that Bono stopped acting like a preacher and dressed as absurd characters, changing often, like McPhisto, The Fly, and Mirror Ball Man. He made live telephone calls to President Bush, the United Nations and politicians. It seemed as if, unlike the past, the U2 in the era of *Achtung Baby* and the *Zoo TV Tour* preferred experiencing and manifesting contradictions rather than giving the public answers. The band spoke to Gino Castaldo for an article, in the Italian newspaper *La Repubblica*, that was published on May 22, 1992: "Yes, that's true," responded The Edge. "It is a reflection of what we see around us. The world is in complete chaos.

102 A pass for the after show party of the *Zoo TV Tour* in 1993, with the colorful iconic Trabant that appeared on the stage.

103 Bono in make-up before going on stage as McPhisto, at the Feijenoord stadium in Rotterdam in 1993.

Values and ideologies are in a state of flux. Nothing is absolute, clear, or black or white; everything is gray and it seems like it's impossible to find a clear path in front of us. Communism was a great idea on paper, but it's shown to be a disaster; spirituality needs to be totally rethought. We have to deal with this and the show is about facing these ideas, even without reaching a solution, also because it would be difficult to find one today. It is better to explore the contradictions we find in ourselves and see around us. The "Zoo TV" we call to mind in the record and the concert is the culmination of this exploration." Adam Clayton spoke up to clarify: "When we started, we were really influenced by Picasso's *Guernica*. Seeing the Gulf War on television, it seemed surreal, it was as if they weren't really talking about people who were dying; it was absurd, like virtual reality." The Edge interrupted him, "Yea, they were talking about cruise missiles in the street, it was theatrical. The horror of the war seemed like it had become a daily show, normal television entertainment. In our show, we took ordinary Trabants, modest cars, and tried to put them in something special, beautiful, and unexpected, just like we did with some of the video images that are disturbing, they're trivial so that the ordinary and mundane become something special, extraordinary, and amazing."

Clayton added, "That's why it was *Guernica*, because the only sane reaction to what is happening is madness; it's almost comical, funny, but horrible at the same time. Picasso didn't try to capture the horror as it was realistically; he tried to show us the madness." *But it seems that today evaluating yourselves with these contradictions, you learn to let go, and be more open.* "The words to 'Even Better than the Real Thing' come to mind. When it says 'We'll slide down the surface of things', meaning you shouldn't look too closely at things, but take them at face value. Sometimes it's funny, and this is what rock 'n' roll is about at a certain point. It's also about fun, entertainment and it doesn't always have to have meaning to be valid," responded The Edge. *Rock has always – or at least since Elvis until today – experienced a delicate balance between art and entertainment. Do you prefer considering yourselves artists or entertainers?* "We try to be both and it's another one of the contradictions we have to learn to face.

104 and 105 U2 wore big caricature masks of their likenesses on stage, and were brought on stage inside big boxes during the *Zoo TV Tour*.

1990–2000

106 Bono at a *Zoo TV Tour* concert in Wembley in 1993.

107 Bono plays a Gibson ES-175, while he sings during the *Zoo TV Tour*.

108 and 109 Commitment and pure entertainment: these are the two souls of the band and a common thread in many of their shows during which Bono shines.

Everything about U2 is a contradiction, a paradox. Even before, but now even more so. Our albums sell millions of copies and the subjects of our songs are about engaging with idealism and the perspective of four guys from Ireland. We're a mix of commercialism and social criticism and that is a contradiction we have to face. It's definitely not something we can fix, but I think this kind of ambivalence has always been in rock 'n' roll." Clayton said, "When we go in the studio to record, we're more like artists; we don't know what's going to happen. We have the songs, but we don't know how they're going to sound. Thanks to technological support, we make songs, like a painter paints a landscape. When we go on stage, we're more entertainers. Or better yet, we combine art, rock'n'roll and soul." The Edge added, "We don't want to just be entertainers. This is the difference with Broadway. It can't be eye opening, it can't reflect what is happening in the world, it is essentially entertainment. But, there is soul in rock 'n' roll and the ability to establish emotional contact with an audience, and there's something terribly truthful in direct communication between one person and another. This is the power of rock, and because of this, we use electric guitars and not paint brushes and movie cameras. This is the specific quality we look for in our songs, or rather, the ability to connect with the audience." *But, aren't you afraid of becoming rock stereotypes?* The Edge answered, "Yes, and it is easy to become one. When we made *Rattle and Hum*, we spent six months in Los Angeles, and everything seemed normal, easy and attractive, and when we were done, we were wrapped up in that lifestyle and we were about to cash in our plane tickets and stay there. On this tour, we ironically play with some of these stereotypes and it's fun, but it's dangerous. You have to be able to laugh at yourselves and not take things too seriously. We have a police escort from the airport to the hotel, and that's funny. Actually, it's absolutely ridiculous. At the end of the day, we're a rock 'n' roll band. Before, this embarrassed us, now we think it's ridiculous." *But, doesn't it filter reality?* This time, Clayton responds, "Of course, that is exactly why we are so attached to Dublin. When we go elsewhere, everything seems enormous, exaggerated. When we go home, everything goes back to normal.

They go back to being small, human, and down-to-earth. It's one of the dilemmas of our situation, living in Dublin or in the international world of media. There are things in both environments that greatly stimulate us and there are people in London, New York, and Los Angeles that stimulate us. But it is important to maintain a home base, with our long-time relationships, and the peace and quiet of normal lives."

110 The Edge: the guitarist's nickname is perfect for his strong experimentation and excellent technique.

111 One of the goals of great artists is to connect with the audience and U2 accomplishes this with their concerts.

U2 had done 157 concerts, attended by 5.5 million people all over the world. Yet, between concerts, the band always found the time to make another album, thanks to the fact that they are blessed with creativity. *Zooropa*, which came out after a long global tour, preceded by the super electronic single, "Numb" sung by The Edge. For the first time ever, a U2 song was not sung by Bono and his unmistakable voice (though Adam Clayton had sung a B-side called, "Endless Deep" in 1983). U2's reinvention continued, the radical reinterpretation of clichés never ceased, and "everything you know is wrong", even about U2, because nothing is as it was. In England, music changed, the sounds were different, the rhythms were new and U2 adapted, or rather, experienced the change with absolute attention to the contemporary. *Zooropa*, produced by Eno and Flood, shifted the band's focus to a technological place, light years away from the music of *War* and *Boy*, while maintaining their sentimental, passionate and energetic soul. Ultimately, it is rock, with its infinite romantic, danceable, fast, sharp and sentimental possibilities. Bono was alternately engaging, extreme, and controlled when it came to the most haunting, charismatic, and ironic rhythms. He was the great histrionic rock star of the 1990s, a fiery charmer and phenomenal vocalist. The album is saturated in an untiring search for original sounds, especially in terms of the rhythm. Just as the first track is not sung by Bono, Johnny Cash sang lead vocals for the last track, "The Wanderer", establishing the ideal bridge between tradition and modernity, or rather making *Zooropa* magically timeless. The combination between their sublime and irresistible pop instinct and Eno's sophisticated vision produced excellent results, which harmoniously united quality music – often innovative and refined – with what was popular. This was about the direct and simple communication that was always the heart of U2's concept, a tendency of rock in the best of times, just consider the Beatles, for example.

113 To promote *Zooropa*, the band extended their *Zoo TV Tour,* which began in 1992 in support of the release of *Achtung Baby*.

U2 ZOOROPA

SILENCE
=DEATH
SILENCE
=DEATH
SILENCE
=DEATH
SILENCE
=DEATH
SILENCE
=DEATH
SILENCE
=DEATH
SILENCE
=DEATH

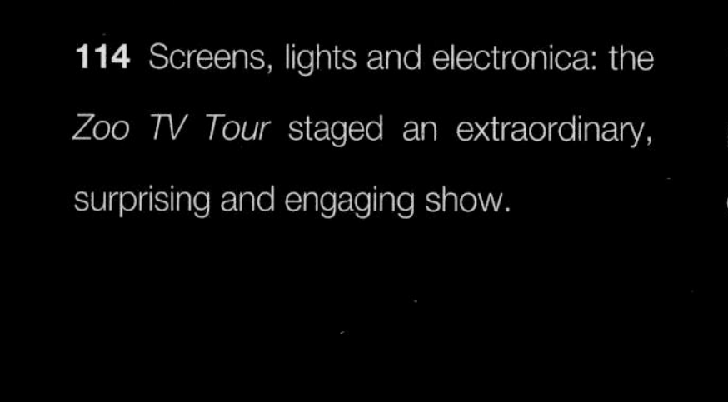

114 Screens, lights and electronica: the *Zoo TV Tour* staged an extraordinary, surprising and engaging show.

115 Adam on bass in a *Zoo TV Tour* performance. A great show played in 21 countries, for a total of 157 dates.

The next four years were some of the most curious in the entire history of the band, when the member's began reinventing themselves, and achieving absolute creative freedom. It led them to make more difficult, conceptual albums, different from any they had ever done, while at the same time, it made them do shows that were impossible not to love. They were gigantic, spectacular, magnificent and perfect. Two years passed and, in 1995, after taking a break for some needed rest after a long run in the early 1990s, when U2 became the "greatest rock 'n' roll band in the world", the foursome became five for the first time. Brian Eno, who had stood by their side for the tumultuous ride of the last ten years, became a bona fide member of the band for a short period. However, the band wasn't U2, but Passengers, a "fake" band that started as a game, to experiment and be free. The band's first project was to do the soundtrack for *The Pillow Book*, a film by Peter Greenaway, but things weren't going well and the idea was shelved. So, Eno suggested the band continue that same path and write the soundtrack for "imaginary" films. So, after jam sessions in the studio, Eno played with the band and they put together an album that is all too often undervalued. In reality, it is musically magnificent, rich because of its melodies. In fact, U2, with the help of producer Howie B on some tracks, gave life to fantastic ideas, "music for visions," as Bono has said, in which visual suggestions, are more important than the lyrics and indeed, many of the songs are totally instrumental. But, even Passengers "parallel" work is full of U2's genius, beautifully highlighted by "Miss Sarajevo", a song that remains one of the most beautiful songs in U2's repertoire, in which Bono sings with Luciano Pavarotti.

"It was the only way to make our fathers take us seriously," laughed Bono and The Edge, when they arrived in Modena in 1995 to sing the song live with the legendary Italian tenor. "As a rock band, we could never do it. But now that they'll see us with Pavarotti, they'll understand that we have a real job. Pavarotti is a rock 'n' roll animal. Actually, opera was to classical music what punk was for rock," they continued.

116 and 117 The collaboration between tenor Luciano Pavarotti and Brian Eno's Passengers led U2 to create the touching song "Miss Sarajevo", which was about the dramatic war in Bosnia and Herzegovina.

The Passengers' work laid the groundwork for the next step in U2's adventure. It was another conceptual piece, that combined the album and the concert in one, called *Pop*. U2 proved to be the only globally successful band that couldn't and wouldn't let go of the desire to change, plan, and create works that aim to be fun and full of artistic vision at the same time. The title could be misleading. It is not a collection of restrained, safe songs. One is introduced to the album's sounds through the thrashing, distorted and aggressive sounds of "Discotheque." If we were in a club, like the title of the song suggests, mutants, delinquents and rocker cosmonauts would be the ones dancing. If anything, *Pop* indicates a meeting ground, a fictional town square where many genres in the technological West meet echoes, soundtracks of tribal slag, and ghosts of the collective imagination. As with *Achtung Baby*, Bono and the band were simultaneously aware of at least three stages: the past, present and future. It sounds simple, but upon closer inspection, it was just what was missing from most of contemporary pop. So, the key was to redefine pop, which is, incidentally, one of the key terms of our times. Brian Eno didn't produce it and it is obvious. But U2 learned from the great thinker. The music is an overlap of very different sound levels that are well-integrated by their precise musical placement in space, which was one of Eno's longtime obsessions.

In many pieces, this lack of order goes so far as to give the exact feeling of being at different distances. The voice and some of the instruments are in the foreground. The guitar is right behind the voice, just one step ahead in rhythm, and then in the background, there are ebbs and flows, true "landscapes" built with sound. The new producer Flood, and his "partner" Howie B, brought sharper rhythms and a lot of samples that made the sound rich and dense. There are sound blips and interference, splotches of color, noise, rhythms and melodies that are so compact, it gives off a sensation that is increasingly rare nowadays. It is a record that needs to be listened to often and will perhaps endure the test of time before it is completely absorbed.

"The structure of the album is pop, but the sound isn't. It is our most personal record, it is fun and difficult at the same time. *Achtung Baby* was made for the heart, *Zooropa* for the mind. This record is for the soul. The records we did before were well thought out, this one is more about instinct than intellect and there are songs with more direct lyrics. The music has everything there is around us. Pop is the sound of a champagne bottle opening, the sound of toy gun. It's not necessarily a reference to music. I'd be very careful about calling it pop, also because time will tell us if it's valid or not. What is important to us is to say that art is still art; there isn't a higher or lower art. Theatre is not more 'artistic' than a song by Brian Wilson. Music is important in the lives of people. You can read books two or three times, you can watch films again, but songs live inside us and around us. They are part of life. And, it's a great form of art that doesn't seem like art. And that is the beauty of it," said Bono.

119 *Pop* came out in 1997 and was a new musical venture for the band, which once again found a new sound and music.

U2
POP

At 35, Bono came to grips with his age. He had been married since 1982, had a family, and children. "One of the most important obligations I have to my children is to not be part of a mediocre band. Joking aside, when I became a father, when I first saw my daughter, I knew that I would do tremendous things to protect her life, I could even kill for her. And, I changed a lot. I didn't give up that part of me that is irregular, I've always been a traveler but at the same time, the immense love I have for my children has made me more responsible. I'm both a hunter and a protector. I can do it because I live with a confident woman, who loves to see me fly, and kids who let me be a father even though they think I'm a little crazy."

Pop is also the album with which the U2 mega-stars took on a new style of rock, the one that won over the hearts and minds of a new generation after the grunge explosion. And that was independent and alternative rock. "Today it seems like alternative rock is the only true rock. We aren't considered alternative rock only because we are successful, while other bands which just recycle 1970s music are alternative. This idea of rock bores me because I think rock is something less clear. Rock is freedom, not cliché. Actually, it is the music of freedom, and we want to go back to being free. This album is metal, plastic and garbage; we wanted to take Kerouac's lead: find something brilliant and dirty at the same time. And we wanted to find our freedom, break U2's mold and open up to other things."

Being alternative for U2 meant risking it all on one tour, the *PopMart Tour*, which began April 25, 1997 in Las Vegas. It was a musical machine which, for many reasons, was the most emblematic rock performance of the 1990s. According to Wikipedia, "*PopMart* was elaborately staged and featured a lavish stage design, complete with a 165-foot (50 meters) wide LED screen, a 100-foot (30 meters) high golden arch, and a large mirror-ball lemon. Much like the *Zoo TV Tour*, the *PopMart Tour* saw the band embrace an image and performances that were intentionally ironic and self-mocking, deviating from the band's previously earnest stage performances from the 1980s; the band performed in costumes that, along with the PopMart stage design, poked fun at the themes of consumerism and pop culture." Willie Williams was responsible for the stage design. A giant golden arch, reminiscent of McDonald's, and the giant screen that "seemed like a television nightmare, spilling a violent, inexhaustible mix of images that describe a triumph of nonsensical hypertrophy of visual civilization onto the audience," wrote Gino Castaldo in his coverage of the concert for *La Repubblica*, published on September 18, 1997: "U2 takes on the guise, almost caricature-like, of larger-than-life characters of our time, whether boxers, cyborgs or Texas oil tycoons. Hence, U2 has definitively stopped preaching, with all the burdens of the ascetic and fearless diversity it entailed. Today, they authoritatively ride on the contradictions of consumer society. That is including the irony that they themselves are subject to and actively participate in this society. They criticize the commercial world but at the same time they boldly participate in the glittery glamour of it. Enveloped in the overwhelming sounds and images, they seemed like a bunch of fun, mischievous tourists, intent on capturing the hyper realistic photographs of a global amusement park. While before they inspired people who listened to the moral tension needed to build, or at least imagine, a different world, one that was more just and dignified, today they accept the world as it is.

Is it a defeat? Not really. It again feels like the intense fragrance of a larger project that makes all of U2's concerts a kind of opera examining contemporary culture. It is not a melodrama, or a linear narration, but rather a Baroque opera, excessive and theatrical, full of juxtapositions and exaggerated cross-references. In the end, their story seemed to be the perfect mimesis of the journey of the new generation. The band has evolved and was always devoted to change as an artistic practice and now they have chosen to avoid sermons and libertarian cries about Ireland, and heartfelt humanitarian and political appeals. They don't sing the outstanding 'Sunday Bloody Sunday', exchanging it for the explosive notes of 'Miami', the center of modern contradictions. But we'd be mistaken if we thought that behind this dazzling display of the simulacra of our world there is only a passive acceptance of what exists.

120 The band on stage in San Diego in 1997 during the *PopMart Tour*.

121 The stage design for the *PopMart Tour* included a gigantic video screen and in front of it, there was a gigantic golden arch. To its side, there was a mobile installation of a lemon and an olive on a toothpick.

In its own way, it is a fierce concert. In its own way, it is a fierce concert. This time, U2 reveals themselves, putting themselves on show, getting their hands dirty in the shallows of reality, going through the garbage. They paint the world as a giant market, but they are pushing the shopping cart. In short, they came down from the mountain, continuing the change they partly introduced in their previous tour, mingling with prostitutes and Pharisees, disguising themselves as idols, and from within the golden space of a giant club, they condemn false prophets, banality and narrow-mindedness in the world surrounding us. They no longer offer their passionate fans the certainty of those who have the answers. If anything, they teach them how to live in this reality, trying to at least recognize what is true and what is false. Everything is extreme in the concert. There is even a Karaoke moment that changes in every nation. Opposites get dangerously close and the same happens for musical eras. How do you categorize a concert like that? Perhaps in the future, but at the same time, it could be from the time of the Tower of Babel. Nevertheless, Bono was still there, imploringly, as in the one of the most beautiful songs of their new direction, 'Please.' Bono heart-wrenchingly shouts this prayer, and his voice is transported in space by gigantic amplifiers, as if to desperately try to bring down the seductive curtains of fakery. Apocalyptic and detached, the U2 of today serves up a cynical look at our world, whether good or bad, on a silver platter."

The most exciting and important date of the tour was held September 23, 1997, in Sarajevo. Larry Mullen explained that: "There's no doubt that that is an experience I will never forget for the rest of my life. And if I had to spend 20 years in the band just to play that show, and have done that, I think it would have been worthwhile."

The tour was a success, the album less so and the end of the millennium was approaching. This meant that, in doing the math, the band could still fill stadiums all over the world for their concerts, but they couldn't repeat the success they achieved in the early 1990s. So Bono, The Edge, Larry Mullen and Adam Clayton decided once again to radically turn the page and as they playfully said themselves, "U2 was reapplying for the job of Best Rock and Roll Band in the World".

1999 closed with Bono's song for Salman Rushdie's The Ground Beneath Her Feet and, more importantly, with U2's support of the Jubilee 2000 campaign to end third world debt." The millennium ended and the beginning of a completely new phase for Bono and U2 began.

122 and 123 The *PopMart Tour* had 93 dates, including the September 23, 1997 concert at the Koševo stadium in Sarajevo.

THE ABILITY TO ESTABLISH EMOTIONAL CONTACT WITH AN AUDIENCE: THIS IS THE POWER OF ROCK.

> The Edge

124-125 At the turn of the millennium, Bono seemed to "flex his muscles", indicating the band's desire to stay at the top of rock music.

The New Millennium and Yet another Rebirth

CHAPTER FOUR

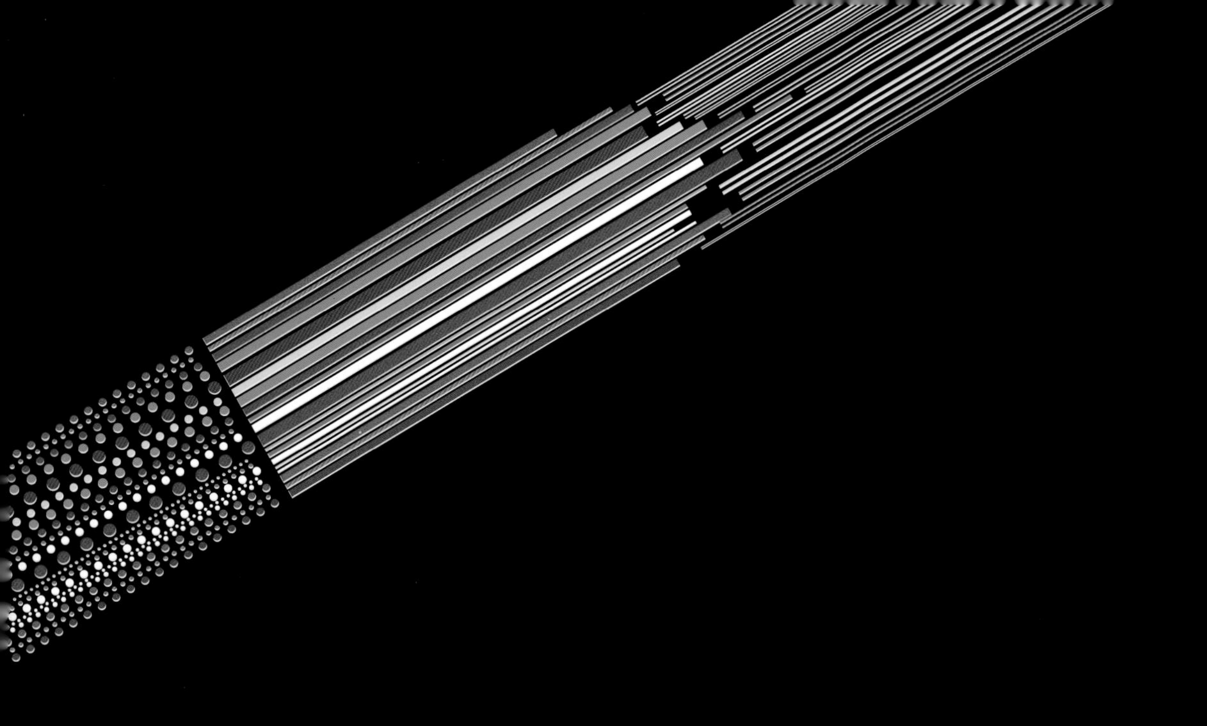

WHEN CELEBRITIES SPEAK OUT ON POLITICAL ISSUES I GET NERVOUS. AND I AM ONE! IF MUSIC MEANS ANYTHING TO ME IT IS LIBERATION. ROCK IS THE NOISE THAT KEEPS ME AWAKE, STOPS ME FROM FALLING ASLEEP IN THE COMFORT OF THIS WILD FREEDOM.

> Bono

The 2000s began for U2 with yet another rebirth, one more change for the band. The new millennium began in 1999 when Bono pushed U2 even further down the road of social and political commitment. He wanted the band on the front lines, and wanted the communicative power available to them to be used for the right purposes. And to best use this power, he tried to get involved in the political scene. He did it in Cologne, Germany, with Chancellor Schroeder, when Jubilee 2000 organized a five-mile (eight-kilometer) human chain and he went to Schroeder with a poster that had the words: "17,099,038 people say: Drop the debt now," written on it. The Chancellor was embarrassed and held it in his hands for a few seconds. A plastic bag full of signatures collected by the organization also made its way to the platform on live television. "Let's see if 1999 will go down in history for the destruction of a country, Yugoslavia, or the launch of the reconstruction of 52 other poorer nations," he said. Then along with David Bowie, Bob Geldof and Quincy Jones, he set his sights even higher and went to Pope John Paul II at Castel Gandolfo in September 1999. He had a 60-minute meeting about the support of the Jubilee 2000 international campaign, which would reach its musical climax with NetAid, a concert broadcast all over the world via the Internet on October 9, 1999, and simultaneously in New York, London and Geneva. Journalists asked U2 what the pope was like. And Bono responded, "He's one of the great showmen of the 20th century. I told him this and he picked up my wraparound shades and put them on. He's great, such grace and humanity. The first funky Pontiff." He is a man of "extreme lucidity; he gives the impression that when he was young, you'd be scared of a punch, and now all that energy is given to his faith. He has given us as much backing as we could wish for." The pope said, "You touch the hearts of so many young people. There is no one better than you to spread the cries of third world countries oppressed by debt and injustice."

Bono explained his idea in a speech given at NetAid: "When celebrities speak out on political issues I get nervous. And I am one!... If music means anything to me it is liberation – sexual, spiritual, and political. Rock is the noise that keeps me awake, stops me from falling asleep in the comfort of this wild freedom some of us are enjoying on the eve of the 21st century.

I am here today for one simple reason: I want to see Live Aid through. In the 80s I was a proud part of the spoiled generation that brought you Live Aid, Band Aid, We Are the World, and all that stuff.

It was an amazing thing, that moment in time when Bob Geldof and a bunch of pop stars raised 200 million dollars! Then I learned that Africa spends 200 million dollars every week servicing its debt to the West. That made no sense to me....

In Jubilee 2000, we want to take the energy that's going into New Year's Eve 1999 and the millennium celebrations and give it a meaningful goal. We think this is the only big idea – big enough to fill the shoes of this date.

We want the richest nations to Drop the Debts they are owed by the very poorest nations. It's mostly unpayable anyhow.

If the leaders of the G8 go all the way with us – and I believe they have the will – sometime in the year, one billion people will get a chance at a fresh start. This is a real reason to celebrate New Year's Eve 1999.

History will be hard on us if we miss this opportunity. You know, everyone who looks at this comes away wanting it. So what's the problem? The problem is it's just so hard to change the way things have always been....

I have talked with Tony Blair, Gerhard Schroeder and Bill Clinton. This idea has support from conservatives as well as liberal democrats. The U.S. Treasury is taking this idea seriously. Larry Summers – he's smart – I know they're going to try [to] figure something out. Jim Wolfensohn from the World Bank – he's going to figure it out. The IMF don't need all the grief they're getting – they want change.

We have half of Harvard working on this project. Professor Jeffrey Sachs is up at four a.m. working on this. The Pope, John Paul, wants this to happen. The Dalai Lama wants this to happen. Economists, church folk of every creed, artists – we're going to be with the pontiff on the 23rd of September in Rome to say: it's one hundred days to the millennium ... hurry up and cancel the debts.

The Muslims want this to happen – the Jews want this to happen. The whole concept of Jubilee is a Jewish idea. Evangelicals see it as devotional duty. UNICEF, Christian Aid, the International Medical Association want it to happen. Mohammad Ali is going to come back in the ring if this doesn't happen!

Throw in Quincy Jones and a bunch of rock stars and you've got quite a cocktail and as broad a based coalition as you could hope for. The sort of popular movement that brought about the end of apartheid, or slavery – if that's not too much hyperbole for you – but I'm not exaggerating. This is an economic slavery whose abolition we're talking about this evening....

The UNDP says we can put an end to extreme poverty in this generation. I believe them. I'm grateful to NetAid, to their concerts, their websites, for helping to get this idea across. I'm grateful to you for listening..."

And once again he sent a letter to the newspapers taking stock of the situation just a few months after the new year began: "So there it was, the big millennium wave washed over us and where are we in its wake? Is the water any warmer?...

The biggest idea trapezing through that concave air is still the British-led campaign to cancel the unpayable debts of the very poorest countries to the very richest. It's the biggest idea, because if it continues to catch on over the next year it will substantively touch the lives of about a billion people, the poorest of the poor, those living on less than a dollar a day.

In 1999, a principle was established that forever alters the relationship between the developed and developing worlds. That principle, made flesh in the words and actions of Bill Clinton and Tony Blair last year, decries the repayment of old loans above the feeding, educating and inoculating of a destitute people.

If France, Germany, Japan and Italy follow suit – and the IMF and World Bank make good on their promises – over $100 billion in debt relief will have been agreed, subject to strict conditions. Jubilee 2000 would like twice that, but for now we're celebrating.

126 Even in the new millennium, the stage design of U2's concerts is impressive and spectacular, as demonstrated by this image of a concert in Munich in 2010 for the *360° Tour*.

130 left On October 9, 1999, three NetAid concerts were played live on the Internet to promote debt cancellation in Third World countries. After Wembley and Geneva, it was New Jersey's turn, where Bono performed.

130 right Pope John Paul II received Bono at Castel Gandolfo to discuss Jubilee 2000, a campaign to cancel the debt of Third World countries.

131 Whether in front of Kofi Annan, the then Secretary General of the United Nations or at a press conference in front of Capitol Hill in Washington, Bono never missed an opportunity to support the campaign to reduce debt in the Third World.

2000–TODAY

in debt relief will have been agreed, subject to strict conditions. Jubilee 2000 would like twice that, but for now we're celebrating. A movement not given much hope less than a year ago has not just raised consciousness – it has raised the stakes to sums previously unimagined.

Jubilee 2000 has been successful for a few reasons. There's the date. It's a one off. The hysteria has reached its zenith. It demanded a big bang, a big tent. But without a big idea, its hubris and hangovers we're all waking up with, not a new dawn. And there's its breadth of support; from the Pope to Billy Graham, the TUC to the BMA, Tanzania to Bolivia, from Harvard to the Prodigy.

Above all, Ann Pettifor and Jubilee 2000 have defined this as a justice issue. A lot of these loans shouldn't have been made in the first place, but kept dictators on side in line with old Cold War strategies, for example Mobutu in Zaire. We had to explain the campaign in terms of self-interest (for the West); in a global economy, we're interdependent whether we like it or not. Misery causes conflict, war is expensive. Preventative measures are cheaper in the end.

And cancelling debt is sound economics when the debt is bad and the debtor is bankrupt. What every moneyman knows: 'If your horse falls down and dies, we suggest you dismount.'

In the U.S. we took a pragmatic approach and beat out the argument with economists and politicians before we had established what Bill Clinton later referred to as our 'big tent,' the threat of pop stars and popes combined. I personally doorstepped such mythic figures on the economic landscape as Paul Volker, David Rockefeller, Pete Peterson, Robert Rubin and his successor as Treasury Secretary Larry Summers. They let me in. Professor Jeffrey Sachs had half of Harvard crunching the numbers. His zeal was contagious. Larry Summers made the overtures and, in the end, Bill Clinton is a star. He saw the light, took out his saxophone and played. By September, he had moved the American position from 90 percent debt forgiveness to the unspinnable 100 percent.

Meanwhile on the world stage, Tony Blair and Gordon Brown knew more about debt relief than anyone. In Downing Street they had the head and the heart for it. With Bob Geldof in their ear and church groups blowing trumpets outside the Treasury, the bureaucratic walls were crumbling. Bold and brave moves were made and now the U.K., the U.S. and Canada lead the world on this issue.

However, we need to get the other major players signed up. Gerhard Schroeder has domestic worries but if he can see above them, I believe he has the will to join Clinton and Blair. After all, Germany's resurgence in the last century was cemented by the kind of postwar debt write-off that today's post-conflict countries can only dream of.

Lionel Jospin, the French Prime Minister, has steered France on a steady course and surprised those who thought he would lead his country back to the 1970s. The French have never been afraid of the Big Idea – and they have never forgotten the historical ties that bind them to some of the poorest parts of the world. Niger, Senegal and other Francophone African nations need Jospin's sense of the moment now.

Italy can do this too. The Pope has made this issue his personal moral crusade. Perhaps most important of all is Japan, the new chair of the G8. Keizo Obuchi can be the man who steers the G8 down the path of promises to reality.

Of course, rich countries are not the only lenders. Most of the rest of the debt is owed to the IMF and the World Bank. We need more from these institutions. Jim Wolfensohn, the President of the World Bank, is a passionate man. I believe he will go the distance if the politicians let him. And the politicians will let him if we keep telling them.

So much to do in 2000...

1999 was the most extraordinary year for me. I swapped sunglasses for rosary beads with the Pope, tantrums and tiaras for a bowler hat and briefcase and war stories with David Rockefeller at the top of his Center in New York. On the street though, it has given me faith in the rank and file protester and, I have to humbly admit, in the politicians who respond to them.

But, it wasn't all about politics and commitment, it was, above all, still about the music. The U2 of the beginning of the millennium needed to find their way again, their center, their heart after having "wandered about" electronica, dance, experiments, videos, technology and visions. They needed to go back to rock. The Edge, who played a new riff for a song for Bono in the studio, was convinced of this. "We were playing in the studio when The Edge improvised a guitar riff that could have been described as classic early U2. It was a memorable moment that gave everyone goosebumps. But I froze and said, 'Oh no, no, we can't use that. It sounds too much like a typical U2 riff'," said Bono. The Edge glared at him in a way that made more noise than any scream would have. "He said, 'Screw you, we are U2, and this is the way I play guitar.' So I got it. I realized it was time to reclaim ourselves. And that awareness established the tone of the album," continued Bono. With that, *All That You Can't Leave Behind*, which was released October 31, 2000 and was produced by Daniel Lanois and Brian Eno, put U2 back in the middle of rock, at the beginning of the new millennium. "It was what we wanted, even though rock wasn't doing very well on the charts. But it was at this precise moment that that music gained depth. When Nirvana, the Rolling Stones and the Kinks were up front and center.

When rock goes back to its ghetto, it lights a spark that makes incredible music. And the world pays attention again. Pop music is made to tell the world that everything is going full speed ahead, while rock does the exact opposite. It is here to tell us that you can change what doesn't work. There is motivation in rock that gives you a reason to get out of bed in the morning. Most of pop music, I'm sorry to say, makes you stay in bed," said Bono. There are songs on the album celebrating Burmese Aung San Suu Kyi, the imprisoned democratic opposition leader ("Walk On") or remembering the violence in Ireland and in the world ("Peace on Earth") as well as electric and powerful rock songs ("Elevation", "Beautiful Day"). There is also passion, life, commitment, love and hope. "Jubilee 2000 came unexpectedly and as a human being, I felt obligated to do something. But I also tested the patience of the band, who wanted to make this album a year before.

135 *All That You Can't Leave Behind*, which won a Grammy award for Album of the Year, was banned in Myanmar, the home of Burmese political leader and Nobel Prize winner Aung San Suu Kyi. The song "Walk On" is dedicated to her.

U2 ALL THAT YOU CAN'T LEAVE BEHIND

2000-TODAY

U2 has always been a band that looked beyond the music. We care about spirituality. We look closely at the world around us. Our music doesn't reflect just the state of our souls, but that of the entire world. We walk alongside, live among, and share things with other human beings. This is the best thing about being part of U2," said Bono.

The tour for the album was more powerful and less technology-ridden than their earlier tours; it wasn't as over the top or spectacular. It was more about the music, as if the "new" life of the band was, essentially, to get their "old" life back. After spending the entire 1990s looking to lose the U2 sound, the foursome went back to it. The tour, with a smaller set than usual, marked the return of the band to stadiums with a heart-shaped stage that eliminated as much distance as possible between them and the audience. The most exciting concerts were at Slane Castle, close to Dublin, the first concert after the death of Bono's father. The September 11, 2001, terrorist attacks in New York changed the tone of the concerts, especially during the American leg of the tour. "We were the first to play at Madison Square Garden after 9/11. And when we sang 'Where the Streets Have no Name' the lights came up and we saw 20,000 people in tears, the emotion was crazy. It was an amazing moment," remembered Bono.

136-137 The secondary stage in the form of a heart was the symbol of the *Elevation Tour* and allowed for more direct contact between the band and the audience.

138 and 139 European dates for the *Elevation Tour* included three concerts in Arnhem, Holland in the summer of 2001. Soon after, the 9/11 terrorist attacks shocked the world. U2 was the first band to perform in the U.S. after the tragic events.

140 and 141 top U2 were guests on the *Tonight Show*, hosted by Jay Leno on November 22, 2001.

141 center and bottom Some moments from the *Elevation Tour* in the U.S.: the first date in Florida (center) and Las Vegas in November.

WHEN ROCK GOES BACK TO ITS GHETTO,
IT LIGHTS A SPARK THAT MAKES
INCREDIBLE MUSIC. AND THE WORLD
PAYS ATTENTION AGAIN.

> Bono

2000-TODAY

142 Increasingly active on the political and social scene, Bono met Bill Gates, the owner of Microsoft. They started a series of initiatives against poverty in Africa.

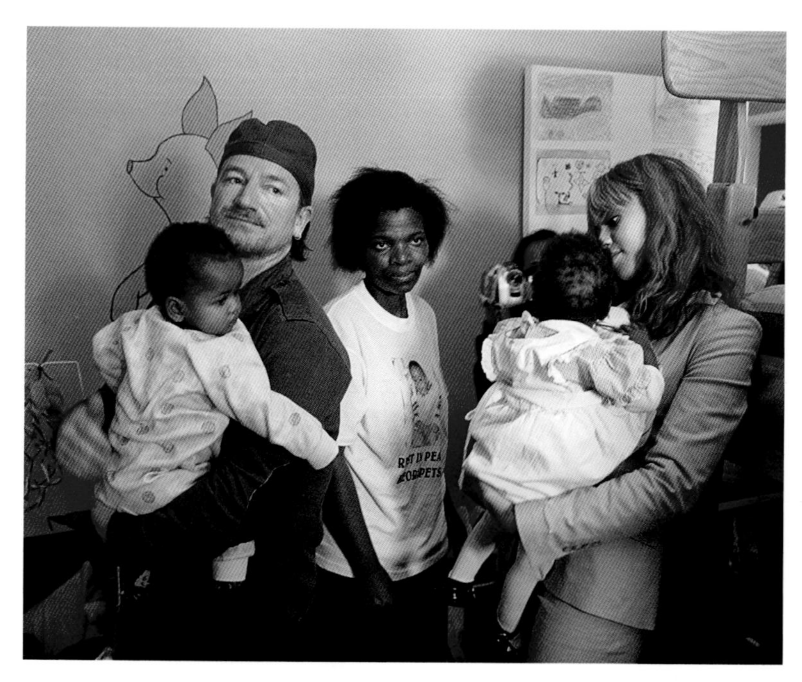

But the "old" life couldn't come back anymore. Bono's "public figure" took on a more important political role, also because he diligently continued his campaign to reduce the debt of Third World countries, meeting with anyone willing to give a hand. For example, he was able to achieve an historic outcome in May 2002, when he accompanied Paul O'Neill – the ex-president of Alcoa, the American multinational company, Secretary of the Treasury during the Bush administration, and hawk of Neo-liberalism and free economy, who had always been skeptical of the effectiveness of helping developing countries – to Africa.

Bono decided to face the most serious obstacle, turning directly to the Bush administration. After obtaining the approval (with limited results) of leaders of the Leftist world, from Bill Clinton to Tony Blair, the rock star broke through with the American right, relying on the religious feelings of its electorate. Even a hawk like Republican Senator Jesse Helms, declared himself, "converted by Bono." He was a proud adversary of helping the Third World, calling it a useless waste of resources, a "trough" for bloody dictators, yet encouraged by Bono, Senator Helms pressured Bush to give 500 million dollars in additional funds to treat African children with AIDS. In March, when President George W. Bush announced the five billion dollars a year in U.S. funding for development, Bono was right by his side. In the same period, Bill Gates, the founder of Microsoft and the richest man in the world, announced their joint effort to finance new projects against poverty in Africa. At the second annual Forbes 400 Summit on Philanthropy, Bill Gates talked about their first meeting, "Yea, we have a mutual friend, Paul Allen, and Paul said to me several times, 'You know, Bono is really serious about poverty and the stuff you're working on; you should talk to him.' And I have to admit, I did not make it a priority. And then there was a Davos [meeting] that was in New York after 9/11, so Bono, Bill Clinton and I met, and I was kind of amazed that he actually knew what he was talking about and had a real commitment to making things happen. It was phenomenal. Ever since then we've been big partners in crime."

143 The AIDS epidemic compelled Bono to do something about the tragic situation of children in a nation hit as hard as South Africa. In the image on the left, the singer visited an orphanage with pop star Beyoncé.

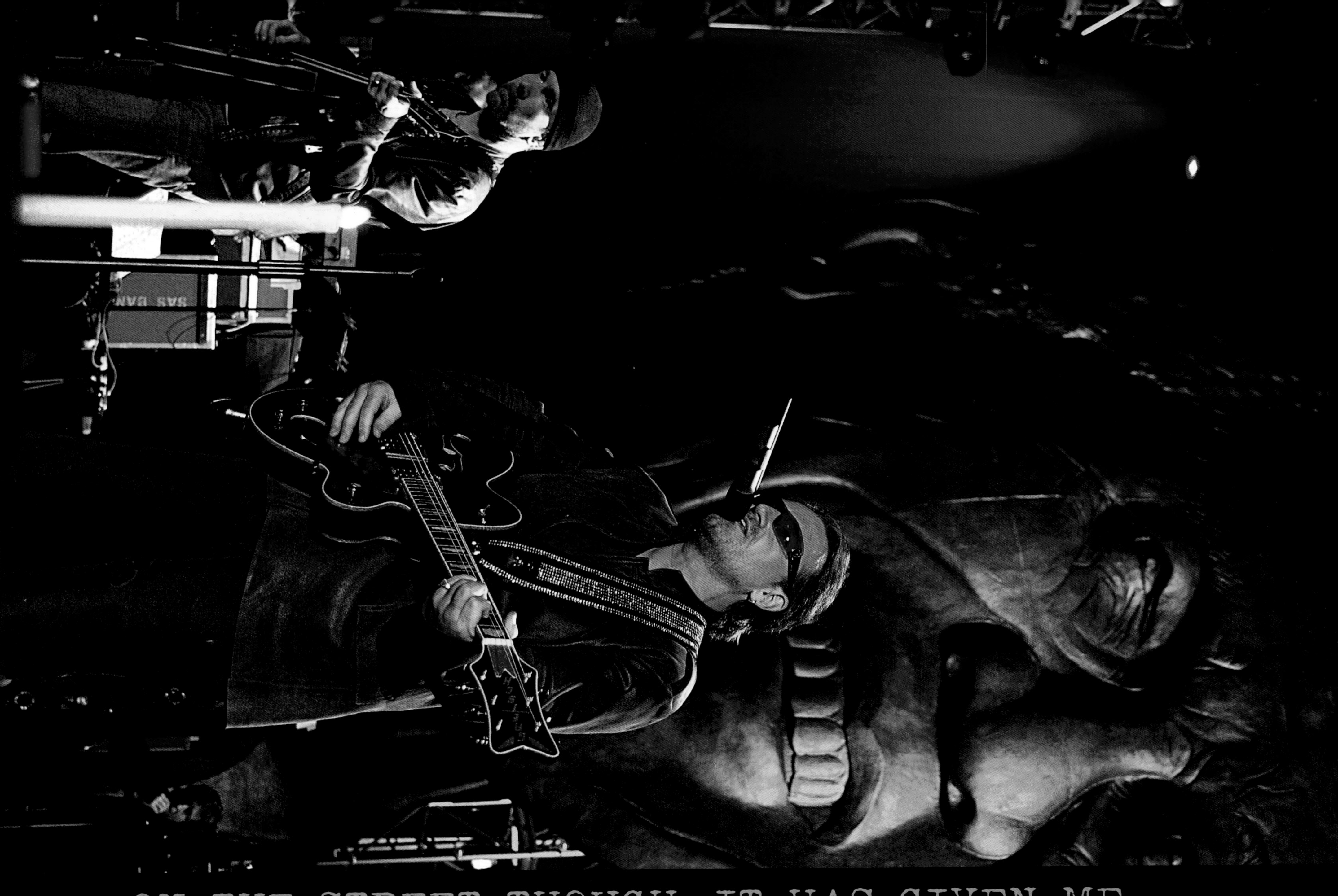

ON THE STREET THOUGH, IT HAS GIVEN ME
FAITH IN THE RANK AND FILE PROTESTER.

> Bono

144 and 145 "46664: Give 1 Minute Of Your Life to AIDS" was the initiative promoted by Nelson Mandela for the prevention and education of AIDS. U2 participated in a series of concerts as part of the events program. The number in the name corresponds to the prison number (46664) Nelson Mandela was given when he was imprisoned.

U2 spent most of 2003 working in the studio on a new album. The "new beginning" of the 2000s deserved a step forward, a new evolution. Because of this, they started working with a new producer, Chris Thomas, but things weren't going well and, after eight months, they stopped working and the new album release was moved to the following year. At the beginning of 2004, Steve Lillywhite was back behind the mixer and six months later, a new album was released. The promotional campaign was carried out along with Apple, who sold a U2 version of the iPod and the band did the song for their commercial. *How To Dismantle an Atomic Bomb* came out in October 2004. In May, Bono joined the One campaign, to fight poverty and the spread of AIDS in Africa.

The album title seemed to have references to politics or peace, but, for Bono, it was a reference to his father, "Atomic bomb is an antiquated term. My father always used it. Today we'd say weapons of mass destruction, but the meaning is the same," recalls Bono. It is about peace, but also inner peace. The kind Bono needed at the end of a period of confusion and pain after the death of his father two years earlier. *How to Dismantle an Atomic Bomb* seemed to take U2 back to that mix of rock and innocence, which was their most amazing quality. It was "timeless" in a world that seemed to no longer listen to rock or to messages of peace and commitment. It led to eight Grammy awards and the *Vertigo Tour*, as the "greatest rock 'n' roll band in the world."

In December 2004, The Edge's daughter Sian became seriously ill and the band postponed the tour, changing the schedule so the guitarist could stay as close as possible to his daughter. The tour began in March 2005, and it was an extraordinary success.

147 *How to Dismantle an Atomic Bomb* was showered with awards, winning nine Grammys.

U2//HOW TO DISMANTLE AN ATOMIC BOMB

iPod
Special Edition

148 and 149 Steve Jobs of Apple joined forces with U2 for a promotional campaign for their new album and a special U2 iPod was produced.

150-151 and 151 *How to Dismantle an Atomic Bomb* was released on November 22, 2004. U2 did an impromptu concert through Manhattan on the back of a truck.

FOR
RIGHT

152 The band in Sydney during the *Vertigo Tour*. U2 had toured Australia in 1984, 1989, 1993 and 1998.

153 The song list for the *Vertigo Tour* in Oceania included: "City of Blinding Lights", "Vertigo" and "Elevation".

IT'S A GREAT FORM OF ART THAT
DOESN'T SEEM LIKE ART. AND THAT
IS THE BEAUTY OF IT. > Bono

154 Bono during the *Vertigo Tour*, which began at the San Diego Sports Arena in March 2005.

155 For the North American dates they had long LED curtains. For the other dates they had a giant LED display.

156 and 157 The enthusiasm of the Australian audience manifested itself in the form of a wave during one of their Sydney concerts. In Australia, scenes from the film *U2 3D* were played.

158-159 and 160-161 The dates for the concerts in Australia, New Zealand, Japan and Hawaii were postponed due the health problems of The Edge's daughter. The exceptional Pearl Jam was the opening act on the last day of the *Vertigo Tour* at the Aloha Stadium in Honolulu, Hawaii. "All I Want is You" was the last song U2 played.

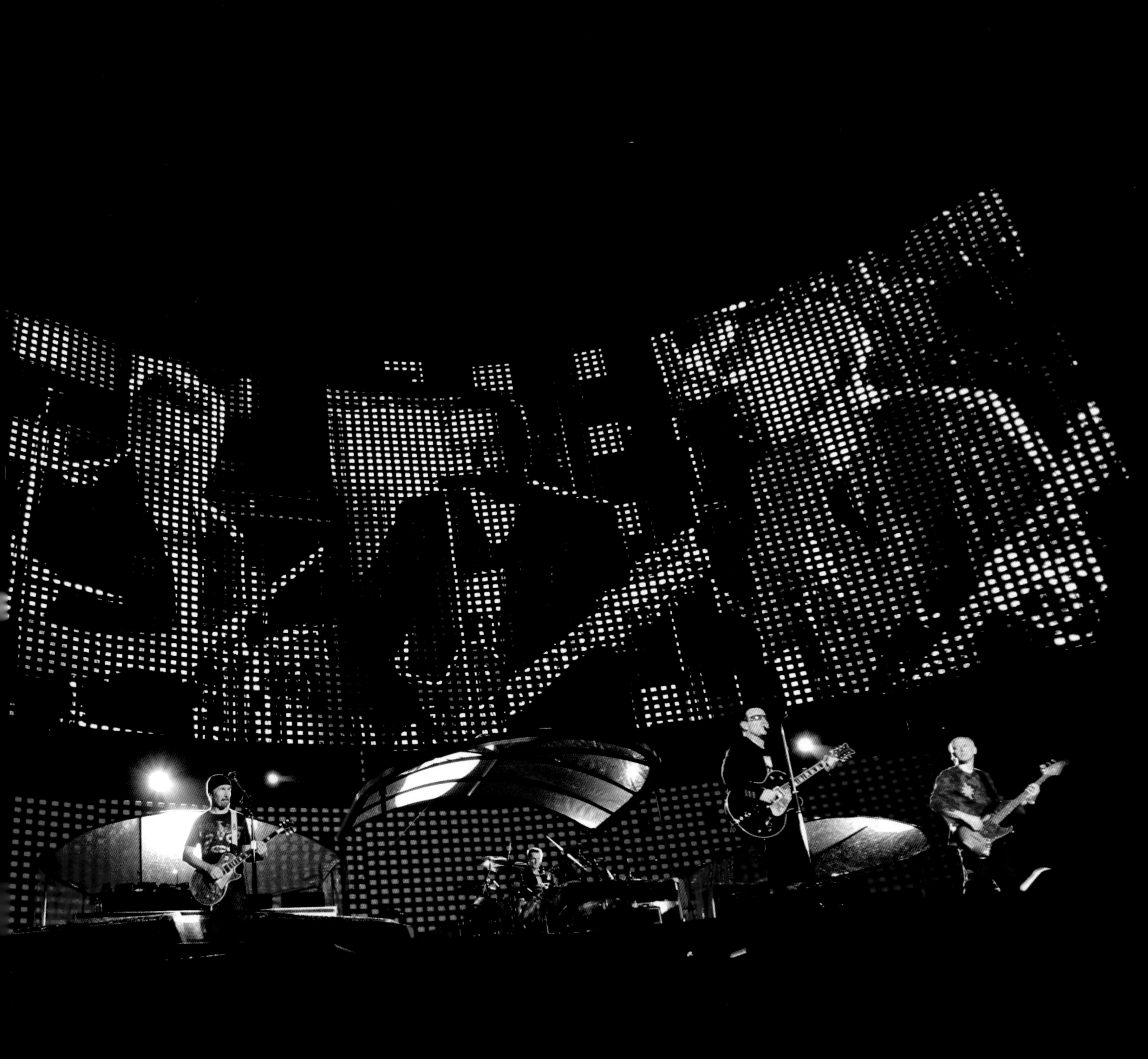

LIVE8

The band continued to focus on peace, commitment, and music in the following years. Thus, in 2005, the band played at Live8, along with Paul McCartney, singing "Sgt. Pepper's Lonely Hearts Club Band." The string of benefit concerts was the beginning of a "long walk to justice", the largest movement asking for justice in Africa and third world countries that's ever been organized. The aim was to push world leaders, who were meeting in Auchterarder, Scotland, from July 6 to 8 of that same year, to make an historic decision to cancel 100% of the Third World's debt to First World countries, double the aid in these countries, and change the trade laws allowing the markets to grow and opening up the possibility for a future. "It can be done. George W. Bush, Tony Blair, Jacques Chirac, Gerhard Schroeder, Silvio Berlusconi, Paul Martin, Junichiro Koizumi and Vladimir Putin can do it. Eight world leaders will be in a room in Scotland on July 8 and they can save the millions and millions of lives, with a cost that, on a global scale, is minimal. But they will only do it if enough people tell them to. We're going to present a plan to the G8 that tells them how to do it. The government leaders must know that if they don't seriously face these problems, they aren't welcome in this country. And we'll tell them with our songs."

162-163 Eleven concerts, with worldwide celebrities, united to push G8 leaders to cancel the debt of third world countries: Paul McCartney, U2, Madonna, Pink Floyd, Coldplay, Green Day, Deep Purple and Elton John were among those who participated in Live8.

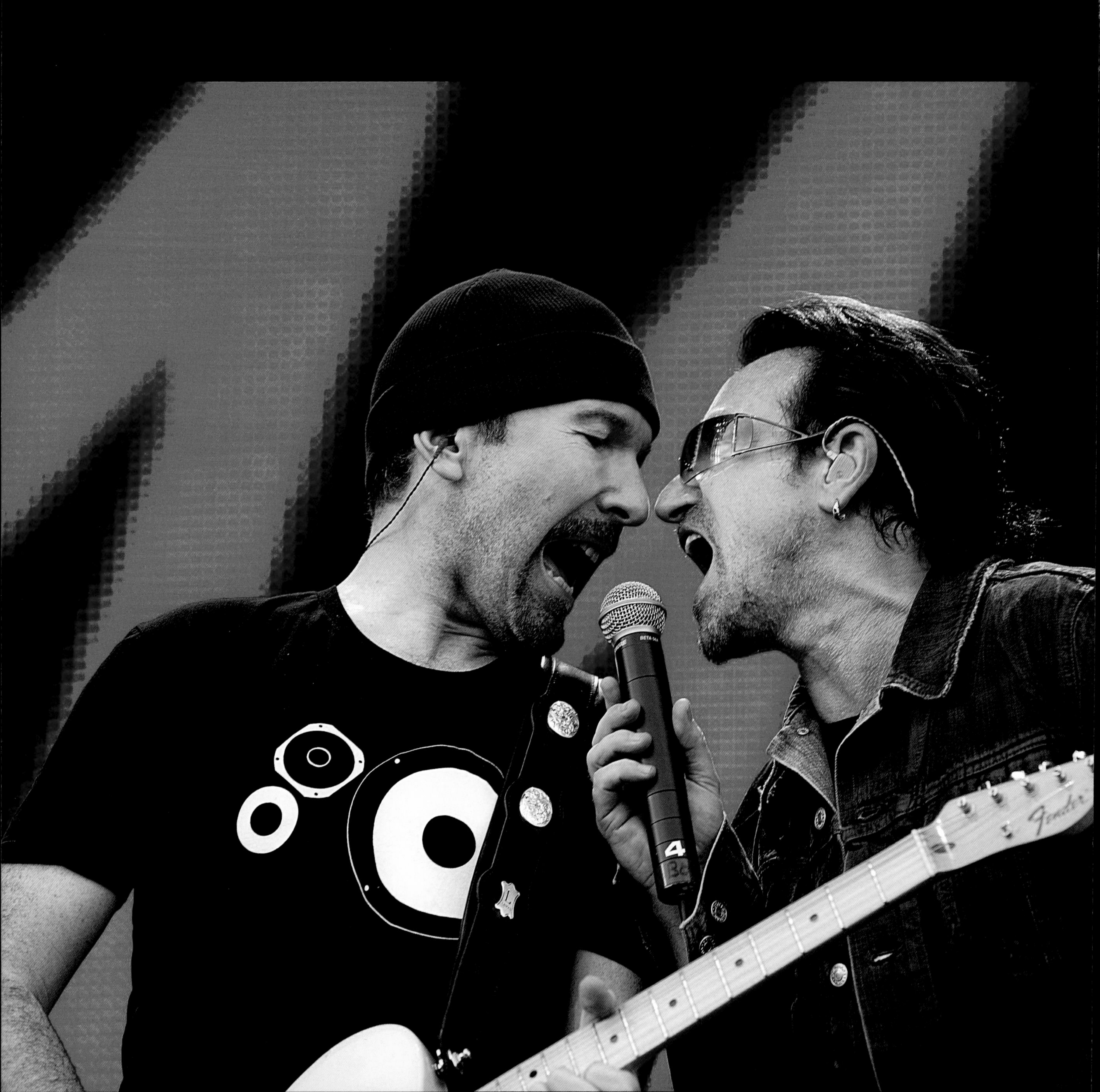
Fender

164-165 and 165 U2 played “Beautiful Day”, “Blackbird”, “Vertigo”, “One” and “Unchained Melody” at Live8 in London.

166-167 and 167 Flags of African nations were projected on large screens and U2 were broadcast worldwide. The concert in Hyde Park, London on July 2, 2005 took place at the same time as the ones in Paris, Berlin, Rome, Philadelphia, Barrie, Tokyo, Johannesburg, Moscow and Cornwall (Eden Project).

90% of our tickets and 98% of records are sold outside of Ireland. It is where we live and where we work and where we employ a lot of people. But we pay taxes all over the world – of many different kinds. And like any other business, we are perfectly entitled to minimize the tax we pay." The then finance spokesperson for Ireland said, "Having listened to Bono on the necessity for the Irish government to give more money to Ireland Aid, of which I approve, I am surprised that U2 are not prepared to contribute to the Exchequer on a fair basis along with the bulk of Irish taxpayers." (Ireland Aid is the country's official overseas development program working to reduce global poverty and hunger.) U2's assets are estimated to be around 100 million dollars and the value of their royalties is estimated to be around 758 million dollars.

They went back in the studio in 2006. First with Rick Rubin, without much success, and then again with Brian Eno and Daniel Lanois for a new album that was released in 2009. The work on the album began in October 2006 and was finished in November 2008 at Olympic Studios in London, with a period in Fez, Morocco, in 2007. This album wasn't the only project Bono and The Edge were working on. The pair also worked with Julie Taymor (who directed the excellent film *Across the Universe* and had won a Tony award for her direction of *The Lion King*) on a musical about Spiderman. They were also supposed to start work on the construction of the U2 Tower, designed by Norman Foster, which was supposed to be built in Dublin to house the bands headquarters and recording studios, at an estimated cost of 220 million dollars. However, because of the economic crisis, the project never came to fruition.

The following year, 2006, the foursome recorded "The Saints are Coming", with Green Day, to support the campaign to raise money for the victims of Hurricane Katrina and to bring music education programs back to New Orleans. It was also the year the controversy about paying taxes in Ireland began. The band moved their assets to the Netherlands to avoid paying more taxes in Ireland, following The Rolling Stones' "historic" example; they had left England the year before for the same reasons. On September 22, 2006, when the controversy grew larger, making the pages of worldwide newspapers, Paul McGuinness spoke up saying, "The reality is that U2's business is 90% conducted around the world.

168 and 169 For the re-opening of the Louisiana Superdome in New Orleans, after repairs of the damage done by Hurricane Katrina, U2 and Green Day covered "The Saints are Coming" by the Skids on September 25, 2006.

0-171 In September 2006, 250 fans ceived signed copies of the interna-onal publication of the autobiographical ook *U2 by U2* during a raffle in a Dublin ookstore.

2-173 U2 celebrates their Grammy ins for *How to Dismantle an Atomic*

TODAY WE ARE A
DIFFERENT BAND,
IN SEARCH
OF THE MUSIC
OF THE ROOTS,
THOSE THAT GAVE
ROCK 'N' ROLL
ITS START.

> The Edge

The new album, *No Line on the Horizon* was beautiful and encapsulated all the soul and history of the band, bringing rock, experimentation, commitment, research, entertainment, melody and passion together. The sound was rich and complex; electronic sounds and guitars blended on a rhythm that was never divisive, followed by Bono, who sang with a high and distraught voice. The sound was new, the style unmistakable and The Edge's guitar playing and Bono's singing were worthy of being called some of their best work. And this goes for the entire album all the way to the last song, "Cedars of Lebanon", in which Bono sang about the war in the Middle East with a recitative tone.

In November, the band played a concert in Berlin, in front of the Brandenburg Gate to celebrate the 20th anniversary of the Fall of the Wall. Emotions ran high as U2 played "One," which, aside from being one of U2's most beautiful songs, was written in Berlin, inspired by the reunification, with lyrics like, "Love is a temple" and "One love, one blood, one life, you got to do what you should. One life with each other: sisters, brothers." While they sang these moving lyrics about love and sharing, images of hammers and sickles, and red stars were projected on the gates behind them.

The projects piled up in 2010, between albums, shows, the musical, and the *360° Tour*, which got its name due to its stage design. For the first time in history, the audience had a 360-degree view of the band, meaning from any side of the stadium. As always, the challenge was great and so was their success, even though the "spectacle aspects" were to the detriment of the more passionate and emotional parts of the live show.

175 *No Line on The Horizon* was recorded in Dublin, London and Fez, Morocco. The Eastern inspiration of the album is heard in songs like "Fez - Being Born".

176-177 The name of the *360° Tour* refers to the design of the stage, which was also shaped like a giant claw.

070

WE HAVE TO DREAM
OF A WORLD WE
WANT TO LIVE IN.
AND WE HAVE TO
DREAM HARD.

> Bono

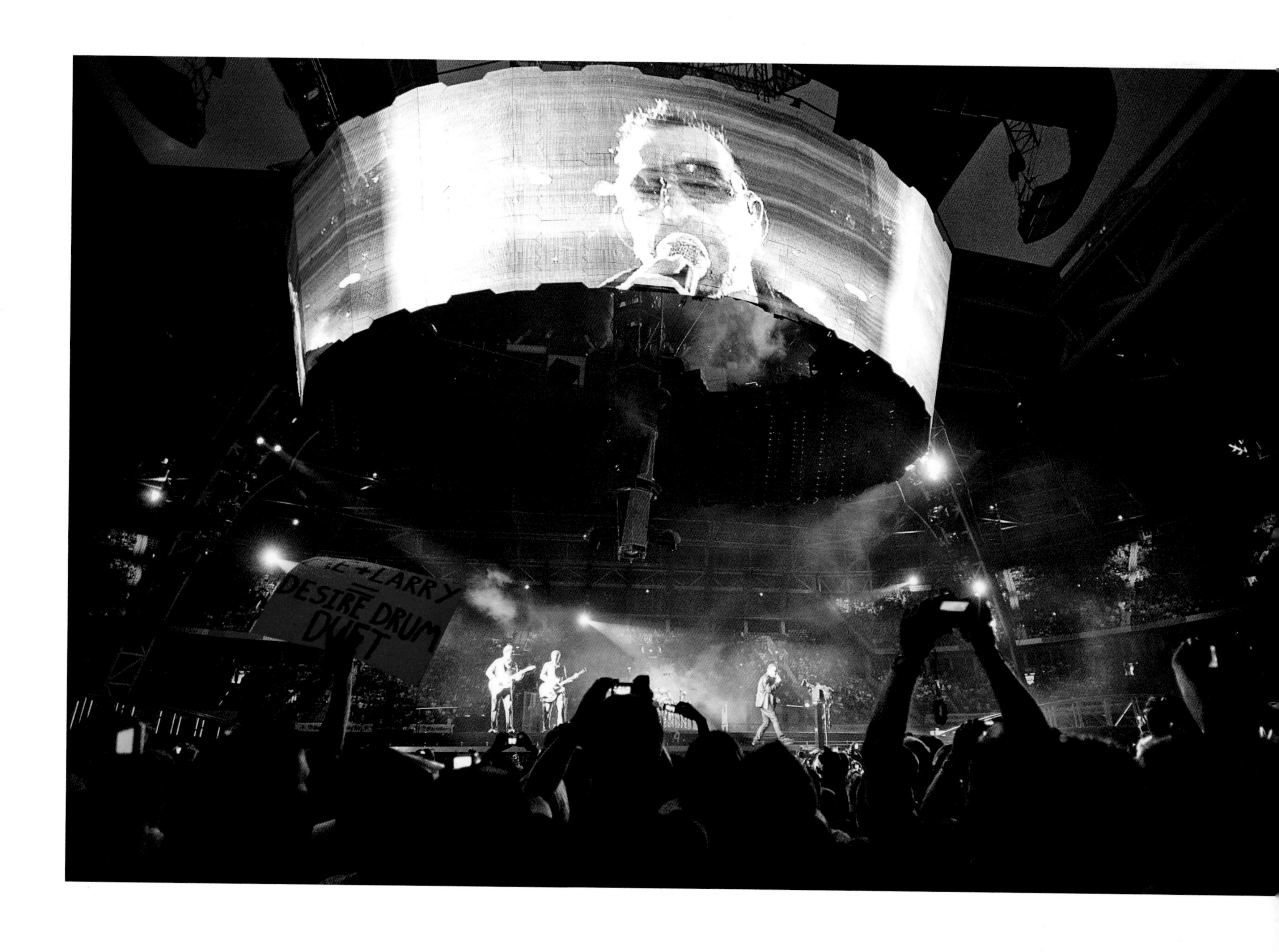

178 and 179 The stage was surrounded by a runway and surmounted by a large mobile 500,000-pixel screen.

2000-TODAY

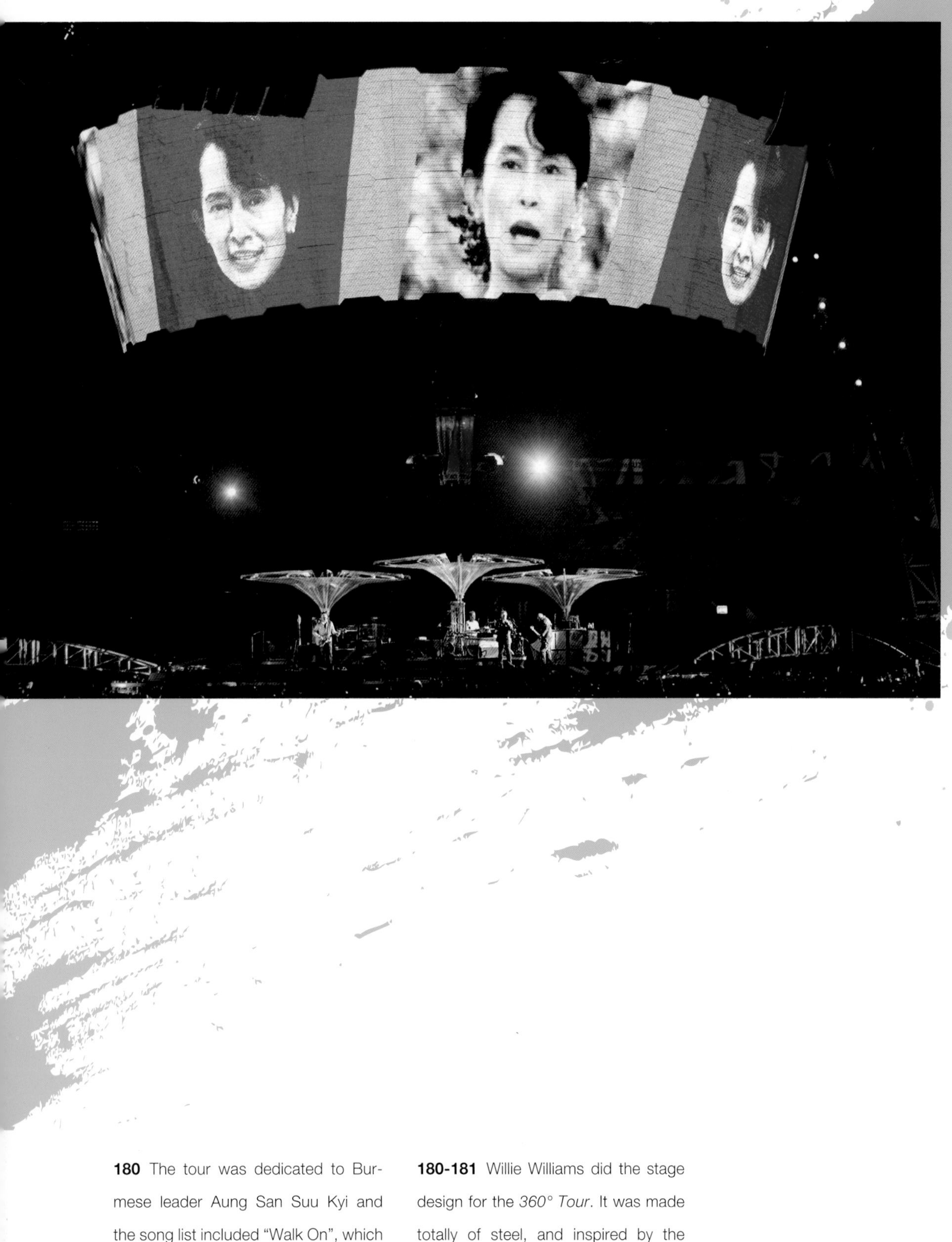

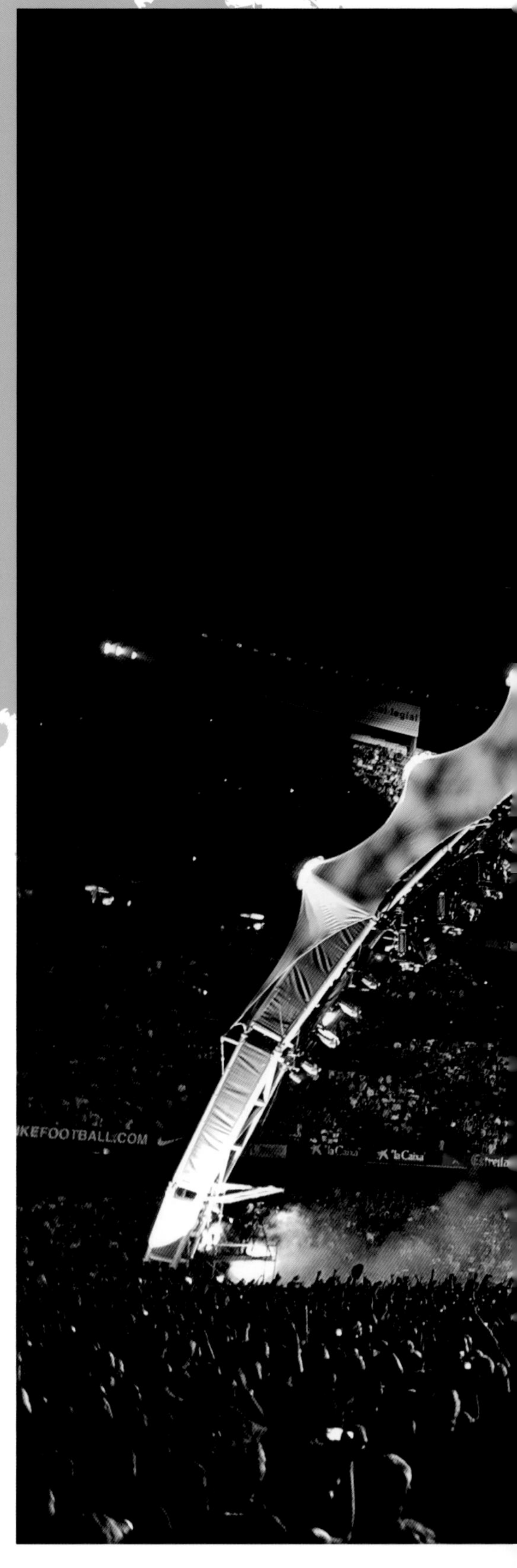

180 The tour was dedicated to Burmese leader Aung San Suu Kyi and the song list included "Walk On", which was inspired by the Nobel Peace Prize winner.

180-181 Willie Williams did the stage design for the *360° Tour*. It was made totally of steel, and inspired by the Theme Building at Los Angeles airport and the Sagrada Familia in Barcelona.

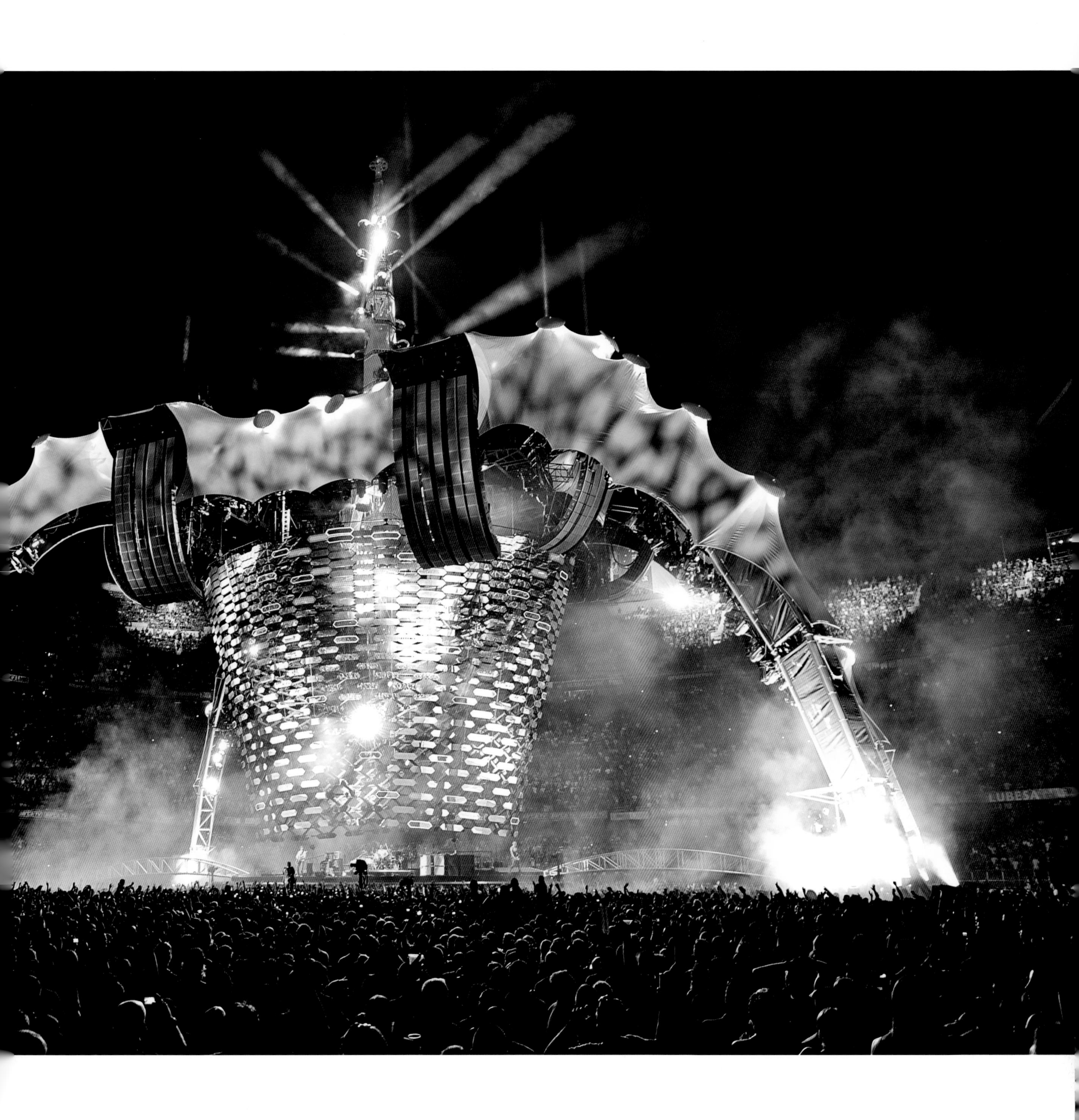

WE DIDN'T CARE
JUST ABOUT THE
BLUES, BUT ABOUT
ALL KINDS OF
POPULAR MUSIC.

> The Edge

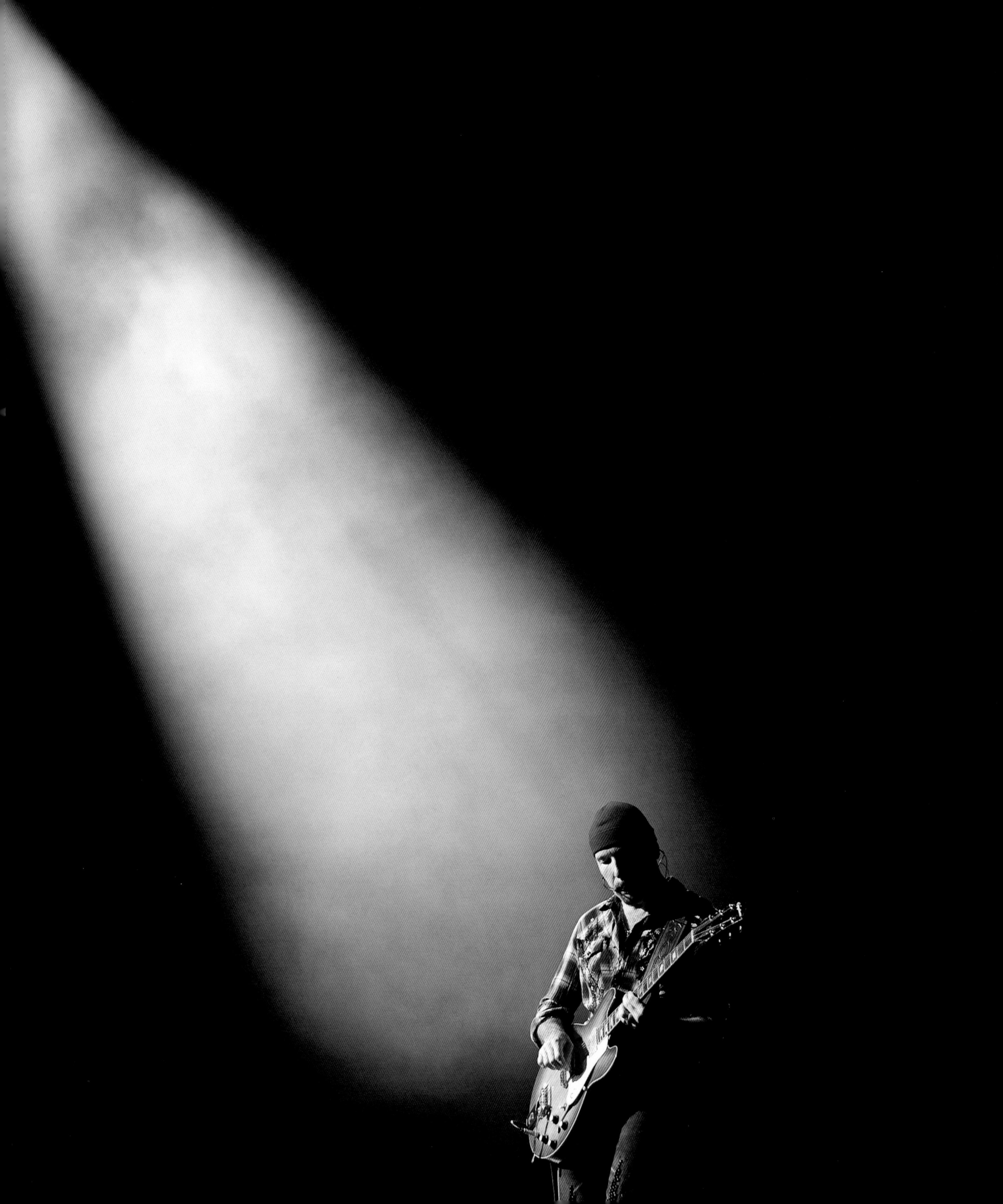

184-185 On May 21, 2011, at Invesco Field at Mile High in Denver, the second U.S. date of the *360° Tour* began. The first song performed was "Even Better than the Real Thing".

186-187, 188-189 and 190-191 U2, in the rain, in Moscow, playing to their first Russian audience. During the *360° Tour*, they also did their first concerts in Croatia and Turkey, achieving great success.

WE DON'T
CONSIDER
OURSELVES
ROCK STARS,
LET ALONE
POLITICIANS.

> Bono

U2

192 and 192-193 Artists of U2's caliber, such as Jon Bon Jovi, Bruce Springsteen, Usher and many more, participated in the concert event called *We Are One*, organized at the Lincoln Memorial in Washington to celebrate the inauguration of Barack Obama's presidency in January 2009.

194-195 Bono jokes with President Barack Obama in the Oval Office of the White House during an official visit in April 2010.

2000-TODAY

IN THIS TEMPLE
AS IN THE HEARTS OF THE PEOPLE
FOR WHOM HE SAVED THE UNION
THE MEMORY OF ABRAHAM LINCOL
IS ENSHRINED FOREVER
YAMAHA

WE AREN'T
LEADERS,
WE ARE NORMAL
PEOPLE WHO
WERE INSPIRED
BY MUSIC
AND HOPE THAT
THEIR MUSIC
CAN INSPIRE
OTHERS TO DO
SOMETHING.

> Bono

Art for Amnesty
and Amnesty International
Ambassador
of Conscience
Award 2009
In recognition of her extraordinary courage and
commitment to the cause of freedom and human
rights. And her unwavering adherence to non-
violence and the struggle for democracy in Burma,
Amnesty International has the honour
and pleasure of bestowing upon
Aung San Suu Kyi
the title of Amnesty International
Ambassador of Conscience
18 June 2012 – Dublin, Ireland
'It is not power that corrupts but fear.
Fear of losing power corrupts those who
wield it and fear of the scourge of power
corrupts those who are subject to it.'
Aung San Suu Kyi

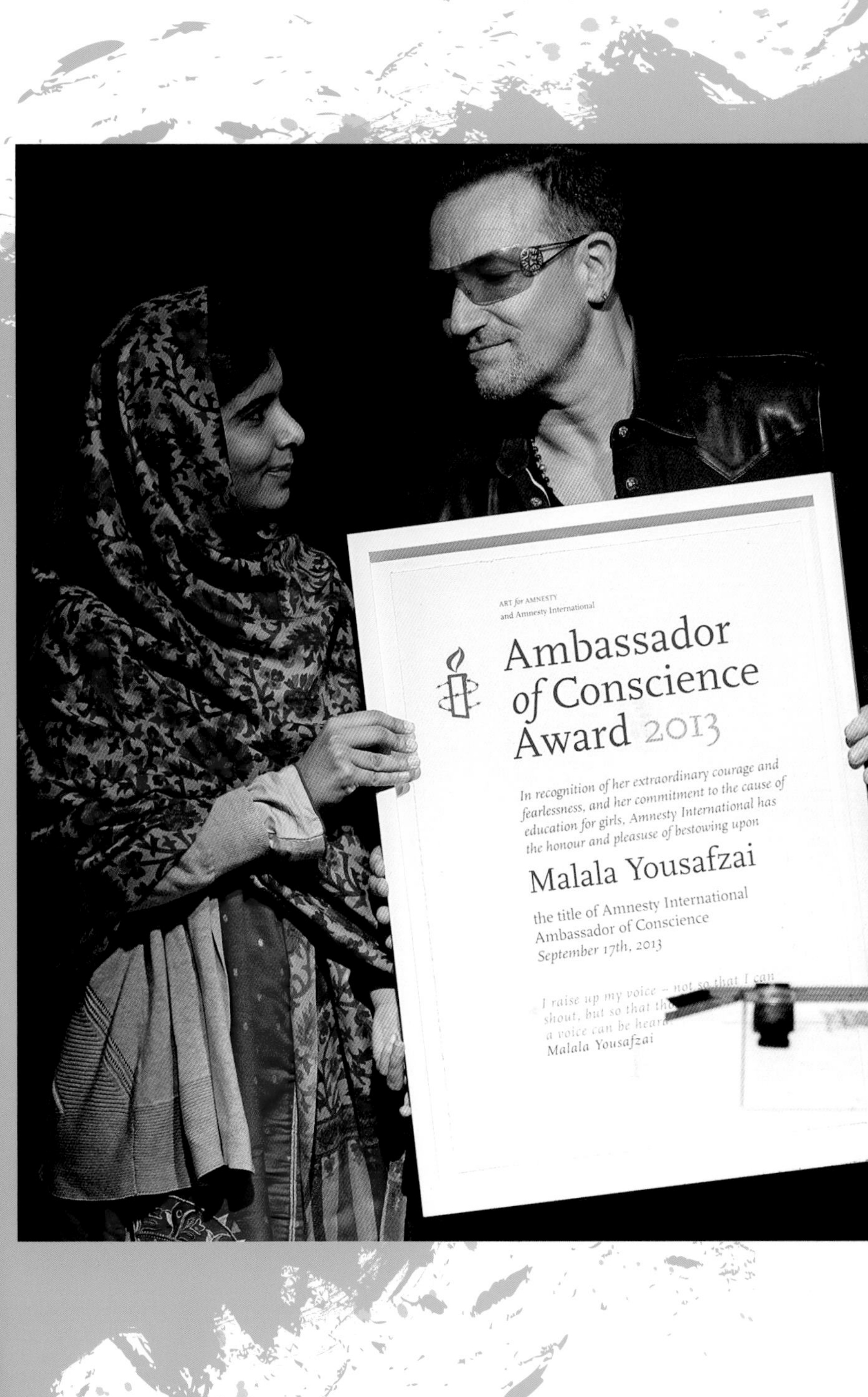

196-197 and 197 After winning the prestigious Ambassador of Conscience Award given by Amnesty International for his commitment to the fight for Human Rights in 2005, Bono presented the same award to Aung San Suu Kyi in 2009 and Malala Yousafzai, the Pakistani blogger and activist in 2013.

198-199 and 199 In 2004, Bono co-founded One, a non-governmental association, which aims to fight world poverty, especially in Africa, and to mobilize awareness and world leaders to create concrete initiatives, like the fight against AIDS, education and debt in poor countries.

WE FEEL VERY CLOSE TO
OUR FANS BECAUSE WE
WERE JUST LIKE THEM.

> Bono

202-203 U2 was supposed to perform at the Glastonbury Festival in 2010, but due to Bono's health, they had to cancel. It was postponed until 2011, when the band played on the main Pyramid Stage. U2, Coldplay and Beyoncé were the headliners of the 2011 Glastonbury Festival, which lasted three days.

204-205 and 205 There were two extraordinary duets at the concert celebrating the 25th anniversary of the Rock and Roll Hall of Fame in October 2009: U2 and Mick Jagger performed "Gimme Shelter" and along with Bruce Springsteen, they played "I Still Haven't Found What I'm Looking For".

206 and 206-207 U2 began their 2011 Glastonbury Festival concert with "Even Better Than the Real Thing" and then played groove pieces like "Elevation" and "Vertigo" as well as big classics like "Sunday Bloody Sunday", "Bad" and "Pride (In The Name of Love)".

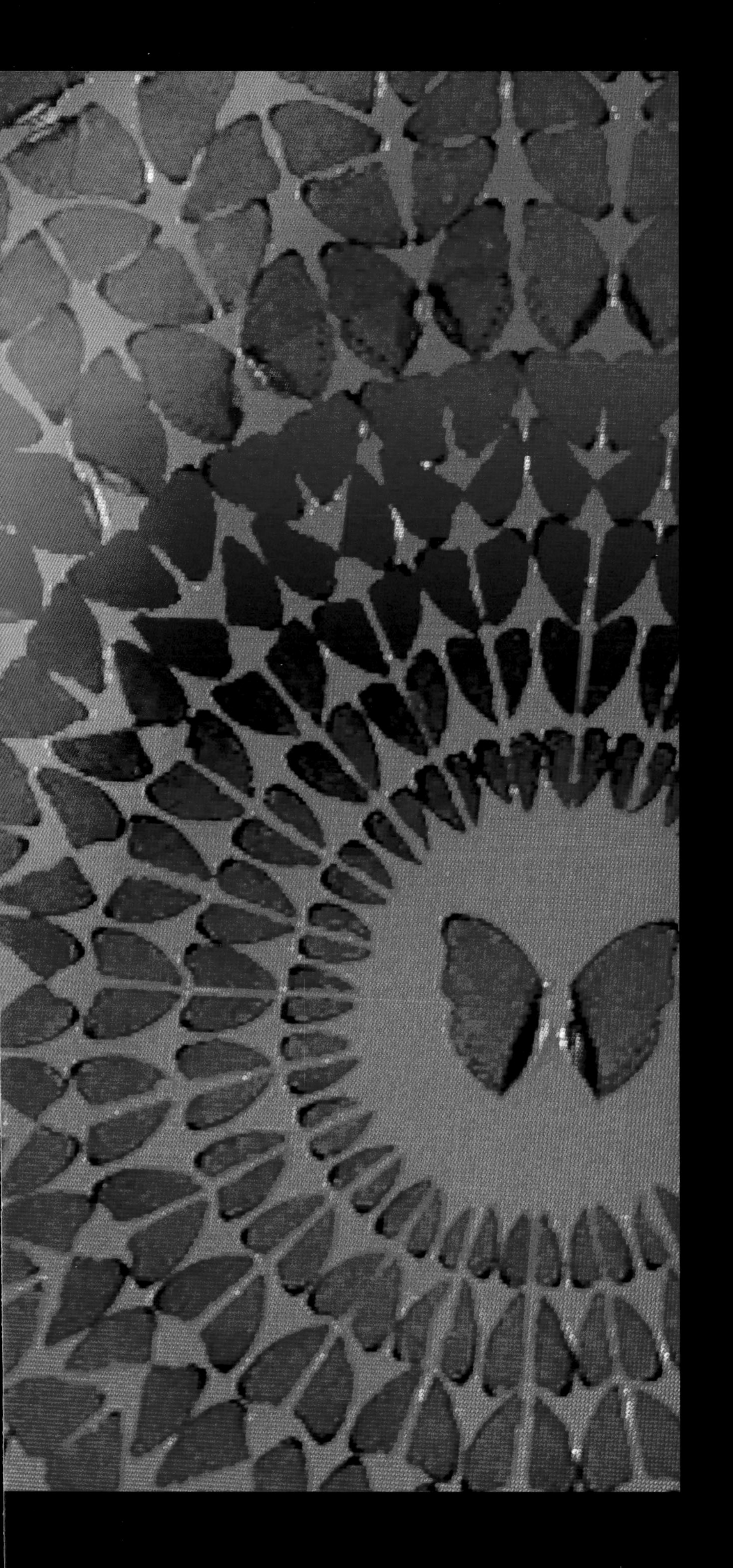

THE SPIRIT OF
TRUE ROCK 'N'
ROLL WAS ONE
OF ABANDON.

> Bono

But, in the continual search for balance between spectacle and passion, between enormity and singularity, between new and familiar sounds, it has always been technology and feeling that have constantly driven U2. The choice to give iTunes users – more than a half a billion people – *Songs of Innocence*, their next album, for free, in 2014, was huge, absurd and enormous. The album was intimate and personal yet confirmed the power and originality of the band, even amid the heavy criticism that Bono, The Edge, Larry Mullen and Adam Clayton received for "Operation Apple" as well as the album itself, judged by some for not being innovative enough compared to what they had done in the past. Some criticized the "do-gooder" rhetoric of the band. Others judged their commitment as "opportunistic" and many couldn't stand the "intrusion" of their album on the smartphones of half the world. There were also those who condemned their tax policies or simply considered them "old."

Bono took stock of 2014 on U2's website. The singer looked at what he and the band had done over the year, which in his opinion had "more highs than lows" in the *Little Book of a Big Year – Bono's A to Z of 2014*. Interspersed with memories, thoughts, anecdotes, interesting facts, and reflections on the morality of capitalism and the future of rock, Bono also talked about himself. He also makes a confession when he arrives at the letter "I" (I is for Irish Pride). It refers to a cycling accident he had November 17, 2014, in New York's Central Park. He was hit hard. He fractured his eye socket, broke his arm in six places and fractured his left hand. He was operated on and received three metal plates and 18 screws. His recovery was long and difficult. He wrote, "I have no memory of how I ended up in New York Presbyterian with my humerus bone sticking through my leather jacket. Very punk rock as injuries go." He had also said, "Recovery has been more difficult than I thought" as well as, "I have written words for new songs, but I have also had an opportunity to look back and review the year in a way I've never had time to before. As I write this, it is not clear that I will ever play guitar again. The band has reminded me that neither they nor western civilization are depending on this. I would personally very much miss fingering the frets of my green Irish Falcon or my Gretsch. Just for the pleasure, aside from writing tunes. But then does The Edge, or Jimmy Page, or any guitarist you know have a titanium elbow, as I do now?"

The explanation of his confession is found under "I" for Irish pride, "I broke my hand, my shoulder, my elbow and my face but the real injury this year was to my Irish pride as it was discovered that under my tracksuit I was wearing yellow and black Lycra cycling shorts. Yes, LYCRA. This is not very rock 'n' roll."

211 They chose a photo of Larry Mullen hugging his son at the waist as a sign of protection for the cover of *Songs of Innocence*.

212 and 212-213 For World AIDS Day in 2014, Adam Clayton, Larry Mullen and The Edge held a free concert in Times Square in New York with other artists like Bruce Springsteen and Chris Martin of Coldplay. Bono couldn't participate as he was injured.

214-215 The Edge and Bruce Springsteen, the "Boss", in Times Square during the concert for World AIDS Day in 2014. Bono is the co-founder of the non-profit brand (RED), whose proceeds are donated to a global fund to fight against AIDS.

estep4RED

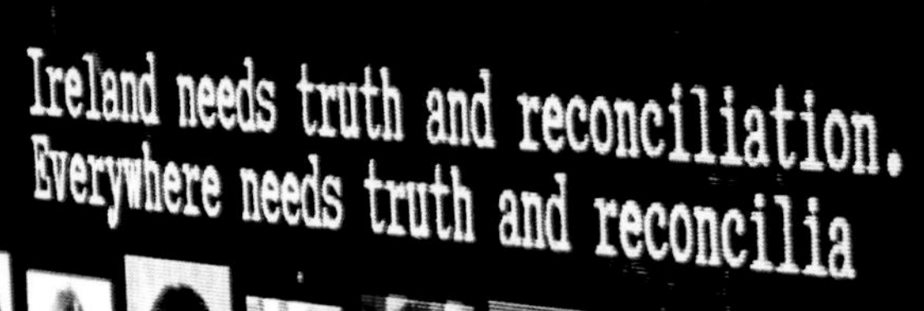

216 The *iNNOCENCE + eXPERIENCE Tour* in 2015 was organized to promote the *Songs of Innocence* album. Two of their Paris concerts had to be postponed because of the terrorist attacks in the French capital on November 13, 2015. Eagles of Death Metal – the band that was playing when the Bataclan was attacked – closed U2's tour.

Finally, 2015 arrived, with many concerts, successes, and criticisms. It seemed as if everything they did was looked at under a microscope and the negative things made more noise than the positive. But had everything really changed in U2's world? Had they become rhetorical, opportunistic, greedy, gigantic rock stars that just play a role, wearing a mask? Could the story of such a legendary band really end this way?

Rock is not a genre, but a way of doing things, of seeing reality, living life, and reacting and responding to the stresses of the world. For U2, rock was never "just" music. Indeed, if there was ever a band, after the groundbreaking punk explosion, who tried to give rock back its meaning, understood as a complex system of relationships, meanings, gestures, thoughts, and expressions, it was U2. They had always done it, even from the very beginning, combining spirituality, commitment and passion. Are U2 the champions of rhetoric? Perhaps, but are there people in today's world that believe a healthy dose of rhetoric is necessary? Or do they think silence is better? Do they take advantage of their fame? We doubt it, but even if they did, does anyone think that talking about peace or debt relief in Third World countries or world hunger isn't important and necessary? What we are trying to say is that the reasons that motivated Bono, The Edge, Larry Mullen and Adam Clayton to stand on the front lines in many social and political battles are not important. What counts are the results. And if even just a few dozen of the hundreds of millions of people stopped and listened to U2's messages and decided to change and commit to the fight, the result would be substantial. Especially when it comes to the thousands of artists who wouldn't even remotely consider worrying about educating people on important subjects like those we've talked about and happily live their indifferent lives of fame. But, for U2, there is a difference. It is important to sing about Sarajevo or the violence in Ireland and it is important to participate in rallies or debt relief for Third World countries just like it is important to show up at the Bataclan in Paris with flowers and candles, like they did after the terrorist attacks in Paris on November 13, 2015. It is important to use fame, visibility and success to give a voice to those who don't have one. Of course, many say they don't have real problems, they are billionaires, they live a charmed life, far removed from the problems people face every day. It is true, but no rock stars in the world experience the problems that people have every day and very few – countable on two hands – care or talk about what is going on in the world, no matter what their motivations are. Surely, the fact remains that U2, after the Islamic terrorist attacks in Paris, returned to the French capital to play two excellent live concerts. One on December 7, 2015, with the Eagles of Death Metal, the band that was playing at the Bataclan during the massacre. "Stronger than fear." U2's music, rock played with passion, that extraordinary mix of freedom and beauty, went on stage in Paris at the Accor Hotels Arena for a concert against violence and censorship, in front of an amazing audience, a city wounded on November 13, 2015, a place that U2 wanted to come back and play to, re-confirming "the life cult." Bono said, "We have to dream of a world we want to live in. And we have to dream hard." The French flag waved on the stage and every song changed sense and meaning. "Sunday Bloody Sunday" was sung in the middle of the audience and "One", was filled with tears. During "Mysterious Ways", Bono brought a girl, Brigitte, up on the stage, danced with her and gave her a camera to stream videos and then bowed to her saying, "Stand up, Statue of Liberty," while waving a small French flag.

It wasn't just any concert. It wasn't for Bono, who was moved and overwhelmed with emotion. It wasn't for the audience, who surrounded the band in a massive embrace. It was the magic of rock, of a kind of music that is made up of the band on the stage as well as the audience who experiences this unity and identity. An identity that the terrorists who attacked the Bataclan wanted to rip to shreds. They didn't succeed, not just in Paris, but nowhere in the world where music overflows out of lounges, theatres and clubs into the streets and homes. "Tonight, we are all Parisian", said Bono while the large screens displayed memories of the victims of the massacre. And when they sang "Bullet The Blue Sky," they showed images of the war in Syria. "It is a privilege to be here this evening," he said at the end of "Ordinary Love." Then at the end of "Where the Streets Have No Name," he said, "We stand together with the families of those killed in Paris" and he invited to sing those who wanted to see peace in Syria, "for those who want to bring peace to our neighborhoods." There is time for an encore, all for Paris, the City of Blinding Lights. And for the Eagles of Death Metal, to reiterate that life doesn't stop, that music lives on, and that rock is stronger than fear.

218-219 The *iNNOCENCE + eXPERIENCE Tour* had a large screen, which was lit on both sides. It was suspended above the artists' runway.

220-221 One of the only internationally known bands that has never changed their original members, U2 has sold over 150 million records, and received the most number of Grammy Awards for a group.

WATCH MORE TV

Author

Ernesto Assante, began working in journalism in 1977 and, in his thirty-plus year career, he has collaborated with numerous weekly and monthly Italian and international publications, including *Epoca*, *L'Espresso* and *Rolling Stone*. He conceived of and oversaw the "Music", "Computer Valley" and "Computer, Internet and More" supplements for the Italian newspaper, *La Repubblica*. He is the author of books on music criticism, a few of which were co-written with his colleague Gino Castaldo. In 2005, the two created "Lezioni di Rock. Viaggio al Centro della Musica" (Lessons in Rock. A Voyage into the Heart of Music) with the intention of delving into the stories of those who have gone down as legends in rock history, making use of guided listening and demonstrative videos. From 2003 to 2009 he taught "New Media Theories and Techniques" followed by "Analysis of Musical Languages" at the Sapienza University of Rome in the Communication Science Department. Among his numerous publications about music are *Legends of Rock*, *Masters of Rock Guitar*, *5 Seconds of Summer* and *The Milestones of Rock and Roll*, all released by White Star Publishers.

Photo Credits

Pages 4-5 MAISANT Ludovic/AGF/HEMIS
Pages 6-7 Dave Hogan/Hulton Archive/Getty Images
Pages 10-11 LaPresse/PA
Page 12 David Corio/Redferns/Getty Images
Pages 16-17 © Photoshot/Retna
Pages 18-19 © Photoshot/Retna
Page 19 © Photoshot/Retna
Pages 20-21 Virginia Turbett/Redferns/Getty Images
Page 23 Virginia Turbett/Redferns/Getty Images
Page 24 © Photoshot/Retna
Page 25 © Photoshot/Retna
Page 26 Virginia Turbett/Redferns/Getty Images
Page 28 Virginia Turbett/Redferns/Getty Images
Page 31 Virginia Turbett/Redferns/Getty Images
Page 32 Private Collection
Page 33 Private Collection
Page 34 top Peter Noble/Redferns/Getty Images
Page 34 bottom Peter Noble/Redferns/Getty Images
Page 35 Peter Noble/Redferns/Getty Images
Pages 36-37 © Photoshot/Retna
Page 39 Private Collection
Page 40 Rob Verhorst/Redferns/Getty Images
Pages 40-41 Rob Verhorst/Redferns/Getty Images
Pages 42-43 Kevin Cummins/Getty Images
Page 43 Ebet Roberts/Redferns/Getty Images
Page 45 © CBW/Alamy Stock Photo
Page 46 Erica Echenberg/Redferns/Getty Images
Page 48 David Corio/Getty Images
Page 49 David Corio/Getty Images
Page 50 Peter Carrette Archive/Getty Images
Page 55 Private Collection
Pages 56-57 Peter Carrette Archive/Getty Images
Pages 58-59 Neil Leifer/Sports Illustrated/Getty Images
Pages 60-61 Dave Hogan/Hulton Archive/Getty Images
Page 62 Kevin Cummins/Getty Images
Page 63 Dave Hogan/Getty Images
Page 65 Private Collection
Page 67 Peter Still/Redferns/Getty Images
Pages 68-69 Lex van Rossen/MAI/Redferns/Getty Images
Page 70 © STARSTOCK/Photoshot
Page 71 © STARSTOCK/Photoshot
Pages 72-73 CAMERA PRESS/Jane Bown/contrasto
Pages 74-75 CAMERA PRESS/Jane Bown/contrasto
Pages 76-77 CAMERA PRESS/Jane Bown/contrasto
Pages 78-79 CAMERA PRESS/Jane Bown/contrasto
Pages 80-81 © United Archives/IFTN/Picture Alliance/IPA
Pages 83 Private Collection
Pages 84-85 Rue des Archives/AGF
Pages 86-87 © David O'Shea/Alamy Stock Photo
Page 87 © David O'Shea/Alamy Stock Photo
Page 88 Dave Hogan/Getty Images
Page 89 George Rose/Getty Images
Page 90 © LFI/Photoshot
Page 91 Larry Marano/Getty Images
Pages 92-93 Rob Verhorst/Redferns/Getty Images
Page 94 Terry O'Neill/Getty Images
Page 95 Terry O'Neill/Getty Images
Page 96 © TheCoverVersion/Alamy Stock Photo
Page 101 Private Collection
Page 102 Alastair Indge/Photoshot/Getty Images
Page 103 Kevin Cummins/Getty Images
Page 104 Mick Hutson/Redferns/Getty Images
Page 105 Brian Rasic/Getty Images
Page 106 Mick Hutson/Redferns/Getty Images
Page 107 Mick Hutson/Redferns/Getty Images
Page 108 David Corio/Michael Ochs Archives/Getty Images
Page 109 Paul Bergen/Redferns/Getty Images
Page 110 Eamonn McCabe/Redferns/Getty Images
Page 111 Eamonn McCabe/Redferns/Getty Images
Page 113 Private Collection
Page 114 Jim Steele/Redferns/Getty Images
Page 115 Jim Steele/Redferns/Getty Images
Page 116 Brian Rasic/Getty Images
Page 117 © Idols/Photoshot
Page 119 Private Collection